WALKI

BOWLAND

Paul Hannon

HILLSIDE

HILLSIDE GUIDES - ACROSS THE NORTH

Long Distance Walks
•COAST TO COAST WALK   •CLEVELAND WAY COMPANION
•WESTMORLAND WAY   •FURNESS WAY   •CUMBERLAND WAY
•DALES WAY •LADY ANNE'S WAY •NORTH BOWLAND TRAVERSE

Circular Walks - Lancashire
•BOWLAND   •PENDLE & THE RIBBLE

Circular Walks - Yorkshire Dales
•HOWGILL FELLS   •THREE PEAKS   •MALHAMDALE
•WHARFEDALE •NIDDERDALE   •WENSLEYDALE   •SWALEDALE

Circular Walks - North York Moors
•WESTERN MOORS •SOUTHERN MOORS   •NORTHERN MOORS

Circular Walks - South Pennines
•BRONTE COUNTRY   •CALDERDALE   •ILKLEY MOOR

Circular Walks - Peak District
•EASTERN PEAK   • NORTHERN PEAK   • CENTRAL PEAK
    • SOUTHERN PEAK   • WESTERN PEAK

Circular Walks - North Pennines
•TEESDALE   •EDEN VALLEY

Hillwalking - Lake District
•OVER LAKELAND MOUNTAINS   •OVER LAKELAND FELLS

Yorkshire Pub Walks
•HARROGATE/WHARFE VALLEY   •HAWORTH/AIRE VALLEY

Large format colour hardback

FREEDOM OF THE DALES

BIKING COUNTRY
•YORKSHIRE DALES CYCLE WAY •WEST YORKSHIRE CYCLE WAY
    •MOUNTAIN BIKING - WEST & SOUTH YORKSHIRE
•AIRE VALLEY BIKING GUIDE   •CALDERDALE BIKING GUIDE
    • GLASGOW Clyde Valley & Loch Lomond

• YORK WALKS   *City Theme Walks*

•WALKING COUNTRY TRIVIA QUIZ *Over 1000 questions*

Send S.A.E. for a detailed catalogue and pricelist

BOWLAND

Paul Hannon

HILLSIDE

HILLSIDE
PUBLICATIONS
11 Nessfield Grove
Keighley
West Yorkshire
BD22 6NU

First published 1994
2nd Impression 1997

© Paul Hannon 1994,1997

ISBN 1 870141 24 5

Cover illustration: Parlick from Beacon Fell
Back cover: Croasdale Fell; Whitewell;
Langden Brook; Whelp Stone Crag
(Paul Hannon/Big Country Picture Library)

Page 1: The Grey Stone of Trough
Page 3: The Hen Harrier, symbol of Bowland

Printed in Great Britain by
Carnmor Print and Design
95-97 London Road
Preston
Lancashire
PR1 4BA

CONTENTS

INTRODUCTION

The Forest of Bowland covers a vast area of North Lancashire, overlapping into North Yorkshire, and in 1964, 312 square miles of it were designated an Area of Outstanding Natural Beauty. Bowland is that mass of upland left rather bare on the map of Lancashire: empty on the map, maybe, but very rich on the ground. The broad outer boundaries are delineated by roads linking Lancaster, Settle, Clitheroe, Longridge and Garstang.

Bowland's two distinct aspects are the great dome of moorland and the softer valley country, the latter found predominantly in the south-east. Linking them is the chief river of Bowland, the beautiful, unsullied Hodder. Its meanderings from high moorland surrounds to gentle, pastoral reaches take in the triumvirate of Slaidburn, Newton and Dunsop Bridge. Other rivers make shorter journeys, notably the Wyre, Calder and Brock that rush down from the western moors through attractive villages such as Abbeystead and Dolphinholme; while to the north the Wenning, Hindburn and Roeburn flow to the Lune, giving us such gems as Wray and Hornby. Then there is Chipping to the south, sat in its own vale and with its own inimitable character.

Bowland's isolation is really a myth: not only does it border the Yorkshire Dales and the Fylde Coast, it is highly accessible to the Lancashire conurbations, and indeed West Yorkshire, while the M6 skirts the base of the western moors. Strange then, that in these days of congested roads, few of those who tear either up that motorway or the overburdened A65 ever stop to explore Bowland. True, it has no craggy peaks or ridges, no mountains or lakes, but neither has it eroded paths nor coachloads of rainbow-clad walking groups. What it does boast is both solitude and wildlife - in abundance!

The underlying rock of Bowland is millstone grit, though it does offer its own limestone pockets. Geologically a Pennine outlier, Bowland is physically detached, and while the gritstone outcrops do occur, the famous edges of Pennine country are absent.

Cross on Moor Lane,
on the historic Hornby Road

6

Bowland was originally Bolland, possibly a reference to its cattle raising connections. In 1332 Bowland became a royal forest, and soon became a part of the Duchy of Lancaster, as much still is today. The appendage 'forest' related to it being wild land used as a hunting preserve, though certainly it was once tangled in woodland. Today the trees retain their place in the valleys - very much so, in fact - leaving the open country to be just that.

Most of the land is held by vast estates, with North West Water and the Duke of Westminster staking major claims. Moorland is managed for grouse shooting, and on the private estates, straying walkers are not looked on favourably. The water authority, however, has a policy permitting access, subject to restrictions safeguarding wildlife (nesting birds in particular) and tenants' sporting and grazing rights.

All walks in this book are either on rights of way, or negotiated access areas or paths. The access situation in Bowland is an ongoing debate, and the Ramblers' Association, as before, are striving to make progress. The agreements allow closure of the areas for a limited number of days from August 12th (the opening month of the grouse shooting season is the busy time), and at times of high fire risk: Sundays are 'open' days. Walks taking advantage of access areas are noted as such at the start.

The most famous route in the area is the road winding through the Trough of Bowland to climb to the old county boundary between Dunsop Bridge and Wyresdale. The Pendle witches were brought this way for trial at Lancaster, while more recently it has been a leisure route to the coast for Yorkshire and East Lancashire folks going 'through the Trough'. On its crest stands the Grey Stone of Trough.

While the deer of yesteryear may have gone, these shy creatures can again be found here, predominantly Sika and Roe: Gisburn Forest is a popular haunt. As Red deer spread further and wider, they too might be seen, turning full circle to the days when they were chief quarry here. The hen harrier on Bowland's logo is a fitting symbol of this wild country so often overlooked.

7

Higher Brock Bridge

Though public transport within the area is limited, good services skirt the perimeter, striking into most villages. Railway stations are at Clitheroe, Giggleswick, Settle, Clapham, Bentham, Wennington, Lancaster, Preston. While two walks are described as linear rambles, other permutations can be created with a little thought. A very useful leaflet gives details of Summer Sunday and Bank Holiday leisure services that reach rural areas not usually served.

Using the guide
Each walk is self-contained, with essential information being followed by a simple map and concise description of the route. Dovetailed between this are useful notes of features along the way, and interspersed are illustrations which both capture the flavour of the walks and document many of the items of interest. In order to make the instructions easier to follow, essential route description has been highlighted in bold type, while items in light type refer to historical asides and things to look out for: in this format you can find your way more easily while still locating features of interest at the relevant point in the text.

The sketch maps identify the location of the routes rather than the fine detail, and whilst the route description should be sufficient to guide you around, an Ordnance Survey map is recommended: the route can easily be plotted in advance on the map. To gain the most from a walk, the remarkable detail of the 1:25,000 scale maps is unsurpassed. They also serve to vary walks as desired, giving an improved picture of one's surroundings and the availability of linking paths. The area is fortunate in being covered by a single map, first published in 1996:-
> **Outdoor Leisure 41 - Forest of Bowland & Ribblesdale**
Also useful for planning purposes are the 1:50,000 Landranger maps, and four sheets cover the area:
97, Kendal to Morecambe; 98, Wensleydale & Upper Wharfedale
102, Preston & Blackpool; 103, Blackburn & Burnley

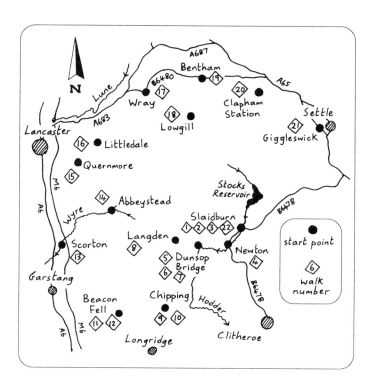

THE COUNTRY CODE

Respect the life and work of the countryside
Protect wildlife, plants and trees
Keep to public paths across farmland
Safeguard water supplies
Go carefully on country roads
Keep dogs under control
Guard against all risks of fire
Fasten all gates
Leave no litter - take it with you
Make no unnecessary noise
Leave livestock, crops and machinery alone
Use gates and stiles to cross fences, hedges and walls

STOCKS RESERVOIR

START Slaidburn   Grid ref. SD 713523

DISTANCE 11 miles

ORDNANCE SURVEY MAPS
1:50,000
Landranger 103 - Blackburn & Burnley
1:25,000
Outdoor Leisure 41 - Forest of Bowland & Ribblesdale

ACCESS Start from the green opposite the car park. If wanting a pint or lunch half-way round, then consider a start from Gisburn Forest car park, GR 732565. Slaidburn is served by bus from Clitheroe, and occasionally from Settle.

☐ *From the car park go to the war memorial in the village centre, and turn down the Bentham road. Immediately after crossing the arched bridge over Croasdale Brook, take an iron kissing-gate on the right and turn downstream. Within a minute the brook swings away: here bear off left to a wall-corner, continuing with the wall to a stile. Keep on the wall-side to join the drive to Hammerton Hall. Turn right on it, over the graceful arch of Holmehead Bridge on the river Hodder, and all the way up to the house.* En route, an intriguing ruinous arched bridge (destroyed by storm) is passed, now bypassed by a modern concrete affair.

The drive becomes enclosed to climb towards the house. The powerful gables of this Elizabethan mansion are graced by a multitude of mullioned windows. It occupies the site of a 12th century hall, whose last Hammerton, Sir Stephen, was put to death by Henry VIII after his part in the Pilgrimage of Grace. This frontage is the nearest we come as *the drive emerges into a scruffy enclosure to the right of the fine grouping of barns.*

Turn right away from the house for about 100 yards, at the end take the upper of two waymarked gates. The fells above Croasdale now enter the scene over to the left. **Climb the field-side with a line of trees, and from a gate cross a field on an old green way to the plantation ahead. A gate keeps us outside the forest boundary, running on in well-made fashion, then as an enclosed way between forest and wall. Part-way along the plantation stops, and just as a first view of the reservoir is anticipated, it zigzags right to another forest corner. Advance to a gate at the end past a tiny pocket wood, and drop by a curving oakwood to Black House Farm. A gate in the corner admits to the front of the house, to follow its drive out through the fields.**

On the brow at last we get our first view of Stocks Reservoir, and it's a big one. Ahead, Bowland Knotts and Whelp Stone Crag form a skyline above the vast Gisburn Forest. The near - 350 acres of Stocks Reservoir were created in 1922 to supply the Blackpool area, in the process killing off a village and a way of life. Salt was rubbed into the wound by taking the villages name: Stocks-in Bolland (Bowland's former name) was a modest community, its cottagers served by inn, shop, Post office, school and church. During construction work a shanty town grew up - far larger than anything luckless Stocks had ever mustered - but now all is gone. A narrow-gauge railway line was even laid from Tosside, to transport materials from the Long Preston road. This extended beyond the site to the quarries worked for the dam. We shall return along this line on the opposite shore.

11

The drive meets a road at a sharp bend by a church. *St. James, Stocks in Bolland was built in 1938 as a graveyard chapel where Stocks' souls had to be re-interred (just the dead ones - even water boards were never that vindictive). The old village church had itself only been built in 1852, and its stones went to the replacement.* **Going past the church, the road enters plantations and round to a causeway at the head of the reservoir, a good vantage point.**

Hammerton Hall

Continuing, approaching a bend a stile on the left admits to a parallel path to Gisburn Forest car park. *The road climbing away is School Lane, another poignant reminder of days past at Dale Head.* **A track heads away from the car park by a wall-side to a corner, where a green track slants right, gently rising through a newly planted area.** *Planting began here in 1949, and recently cleared of wind damaged trees, this initially untidy area is being replanted with a greater variety of broadleaved trees. Regrowth of ground vegetation will soon cover the scars, and small areas are being left unplanted to permit views over the reservoir.*

Following red and white markers, *good views are enjoyed over the upper Hodder with colourful scenery behind.* **A track of sorts is met coming down just before crossing a side-stream. Keeping left, and now level, we approach mature plantings: the posts take the forest trail up to the right, but we go into trees on a good footpath over a stream, and rapidly into a clearing at an old barn. The path takes the obvious way bearing left on a grassy avenue between tall, dark walls. Light at the end of the tunnel comes quickly, at a gate into green pasture with glorious open country all around. Advance on a faint, raised green way to drop to an arched bridge over Hasgill Beck. Across it the track asserts itself to rise up field-sides to a barn and shelter belt, all that remain of New House.**

12

The track continues to a stile and gate just above, where pause to look back over Stocks' waters to the great prow of Pendle Hill. *The continuing broad track is not shown on the Pathfinder map as it crosses a pasture to a wall at the end. The right of way leaves this track to take a longer circuit around the top of the pasture before dropping back to rejoin it. From a gate at the end the track descends a field-side to the top of Parks Clough, but as it turns to run on to Catlow Farm, turn down a greener way by the wooded ravine to meet the farm drive. This leads down to the lively young Hodder at Lock Bridge.* Climbing away, look back to appraise the enviable setting of Catlow Farm beneath Hasgill Fell, with the outcrops of Bowland Knotts high above. *The farm road rises to emerge by way of the white-walled Kenibus onto the Bentham road.*

Turn left, crossing the wooded environs of Hare Clough Beck and on to a bend. Without crossing the cattle-grid use the stile directly ahead, and take a track past a substantial barn. After a couple of fields vacate it - as it starts a gentle decline alongside a line of thorns - by an initially less appealing track that sets off through rushes on the right: discerning eyes will see it continue as a contouring green way. This is the bed of the former rail line constructed to transport stone quarried from the fellside for use in building the dam.

Winter at Stocks Reservoir

It is impossible to go astray on this next stage, for aside from one or two moister moments, a super route takes off along the track-bed, featuring an early cutting. Ahead is the great sprawl of the forest again. Soon the reservoir appears ahead, and remains in our sights for the rest of this railway walk. All 'bridges' are down, and

13

the surrounding terrain is largely gone to seed, but colourful with it: curiously, the *Pathfinder* map fails to recognise its existence. **The point of departure is about 1½ miles from leaving the road, and is signposted just after crossing a beck lined with gnarled trees. As the railway heads for a cutting to leave the reservoir's environs, leave them both by engaging a largely pathless slant up to a brow, keeping left of trees and a ruin to reach another ruin on a higher brow.** Halt to look back over the reservoir before heading off.

Past the ruin a thin path forms, and a modest switchback over spurs and sykes - aided by occasional waymarks and at least one helpful slab bridge - leads to a stile at the top corner of a wood. Ahead are spacious views over to the great mass of Dunsop and Croasdale Fells. **A slim trod heads away to drop - by way of a double-slab slate footbridge - to meet a drive to Hollins House. Turn right to follow its green way out onto a road - a metal stile is found just left of the gate. Go left for a while,** still enjoying extensive views. If Pendle Hill is enshrouded, it is more likely to be from the cement works near Clitheroe than morning mist. There is also a further brief glimpse of the reservoir. **After a steep descent take the first farm drive on the right, signed Shay House and Croasdale.**

Shay House is the nearest, and as a bridge crosses Croasdale Beck to the farm, opt instead for a stile on the left by a home-made waymark. Turn downstream - noting the veritable farming museum on the opposite bank - **but at the first bend as it swings away, keep straight on to a stile in the wall ahead. Head away to the far end, where from a stile in the corner cross a track before rising up the**

field with a stunted line of hawthorn. Halt here to look back over a smashing scene beyond Shay House to the now familiar Dunsop and Croasdale Fells.

Maintain a straight line through several fields. At one point there is a good view of Hammerton Hall, back down to the left. **Approaching a line of trees bear left to a wall-corner, and follow the wall to a stile into a wooded corner. Go straight through and Slaidburn appears ahead. Descend a straight line towards it, locating a stile back onto the road just short of the bridge where we left the village.**

War Memorial, Slaidburn

SLAIDBURN

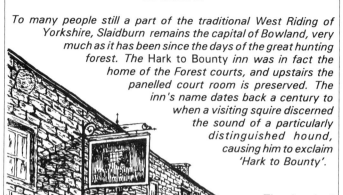

To many people still a part of the traditional West Riding of Yorkshire, Slaidburn remains the capital of Bowland, very much as it has been since the days of the great hunting forest. The Hark to Bounty *inn was in fact the home of the Forest courts, and upstairs the panelled court room is preserved. The inn's name dates back a century to when a visiting squire discerned the sound of a particularly distinguished hound, causing him to exclaim 'Hark to Bounty'.*

The church of St Andrew dates from the 15th century, and boasts a solid tower. Inside are old box pews, a three-decker pulpit, and its finest treasure, a Jacobean rood screen. Adjacent is the old grammar school, founded in 1717, a lovely building that retains its purpose today as the village school. A fine war memorial stands in the village centre, which also boasts a Post office, shop and youth hostel, once the Black Bull inn. Overlooked by the arched bridge is the spacious green, which is hugely popular with visitors. Alongside, a cafe does brisk trade.

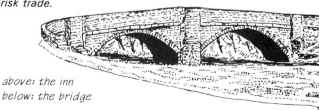

above: the inn
below: the bridge

15

2

DUNSOP FELL & CROASDALE

START Slaidburn   Grid ref. SD 713523

DISTANCE 8 miles

ORDNANCE SURVEY MAPS
1:50,000
Landranger 103 - Blackburn & Burnley
1:25,000
Outdoor Leisure 41 - Forest of Bowland & Ribblesdale

ACCESS   Start from the riverside green, across from the large car park by the bridge. Slaidburn is served by buses from Clitheroe and occasionally Settle.

For some notes on Slaidburn please refer to the previous page.

❏ *Leave by the road past the* Hark to Bounty *inn, a steep hill which at the top affords excellent views of the fell country. This road undulates for another mile or so, passing Ellerbeck Hall with its 1694 datestone. At a junction with Woodhouse Lane, note the old guidepost, inscribed 'Slaidburn, Hornby, 1816'. This is the old road with which we shall be better acquainted later in the walk. Just a little further, over the brow (with Dunsop Fell ever nearer now, just ahead) and swinging left, take the first drive right, to Burnside.*

In these reedy pastures the drive crosses the line of the Roman road running north from Ribchester to Over Burrow in the Lune Valley. The former farmhouse at Burnside sits tucked under Dunsop Fell: without entering its grounds take the small gate ahead, over a plank bridge and up the enclosure side. In the field above rise to another gate to gain a corner of the fell. Up the side of this rough pasture cross the tiny beck and an initially sunken way rises through some reedy sections. This improves into a good path, climbing to a hidden gate at the top onto the fell proper.

A sunken way slants right towards the pronounced end of the spur.
Extensive views eastward include Easington Fell, the prow of
Pendle Hill, Stocks Reservoir (better seen as height is gained) with
Gisburn Forest behind. **Just short of the spur-end double back,**
selecting one of the braided sunken ways. This classy staircase
surmounts the full height of the spur above Dunsop Brook. Bearing
round to the right inside
the shoulder, it crosses
the beginnings of the
brook to falter in a small
marshy tract. By now a
wall appears ahead, and
the thin trod makes for it.

Croasdale
Fell
House of
Croasdale
⑤
Croasdale
House
Croasdale
⑥
Brook
N

④
Dunsop ○ Fell
Dunsop ○ Brook
Dunsop
Head
Dunsop Brook
③

Shay
House

Wood House Lane

②
Burnside
Cottage

⑦

Views open out to
reveal a moorland
skyline that is the very
heart of Bowland, with
rounded Totridge most
prominent to the south. In
the other direction,
Penyghent and Fountains Fell
make a shapely Dales skyline.

Ellerbeck
Hall

①

SLAIDBURN

Just a little further is a gate, and
here, at Dunsop Head, is the turning point, where
paths up either spur of Dunsop Brook merge. *They go through the*
gate together to enter the heathery expanses above Whitendale.

Back at the gate meanwhile, double back quite sharply on a
waymarked path - a stake set in stones sends you on your way.
Initially slender, it keeps to the right of a peaty section, and stays
right when a branch goes left to a wall/fence corner. Quickly
improving, the track attains standards set by our ascent route.
Beginning its descent it transforms, inevitably, into a sunken way,
a smashing walk with time to appraise a distant panorama
dominated by Three Peaks country. **Joined by a wall as height is**
lost, it runs along to a corner to slant away again for the final section

17

down to join the old Hornby Road. Here, just above the fell gate, it has lost its full surface and is concreted. If tiring, this is the point to turn down for a quicker return. *Our way goes left for a level walk during which time it loses the concrete and swings left to head back for the wild fells.*

Linking the Lune and Hodder valleys, the Hornby Road - or Salters Way - has been a moorland highway for many centuries. It is best known as a salters' packway leading inland from Morecambe Bay to the farms of the Ribble Valley: the name Salter Fell, further west, recalls those days. For three miles it overlaid the Roman road crossed earlier in the walk. Around this bend the Roman road comes in, and together they are seen climbing past an old quarry on Croasdale Fell: wild Croasdale is now all ours. WALK 22 makes the classic crossing to Hornby, but today we leave it long before then.

Shortly after a slight descent, a green trackway doubles back to the right, zealous waymarking dispelling any thoughts of missing it. This old drive leads to the tumbledown House of Croasdale, *possibly the site of a medieval hunting lodge.* **Leaving it, a thin path slants down the reedy pasture towards Croasdale Brook. Before reaching it the path turns right at a crumbling wall, to run above it, a smashing walk that parallels the gurgling stream.** *Whilst some waymarking is a good thing, a valley full of yellow topped sticks detracts strongly from the untamed aspect of this lovely country.* **When a wall crosses the beck, a gate in it gives access to a farm bridge, which is crossed to resume downstream.**

Ellerbeck Hall

The path engages a particularly grand section, the beck briefly becoming tightly enclosed. *On traversing the bank note the tilted rock strata, and a final view back upstream.*

Around the corner a green rake rises to a brow, along which Croasdale House is quickly espied. Descending towards it, a track forms to cross a tiny stream and runs along to the farm. Its drive leads out through the fields, but after passing through a gate past a stream, leave the drive and angle towards the beck to find a stile in the far corner. Continue downstream to emerge onto the drive to Shay House Farm.

Old guidepost on Wood House Lane

Don't cross the bridge, but take a stile opposite by a home-made waymark. Turn downstream *- noting the veritable farming museum on the opposite bank - but at the first bend as it swings away, keep straight on to a stile in the wall ahead. Head away to the far end, and from a stile in the corner rise up the field with a stunted line of hawthorn.* Halt here to look back over a glorious scene beyond Shay House to the fells of our day's exertions.

Maintain a straight line through several fields: at one point there is a good view of Hammerton Hall (visited on WALK 1), back down to the left. Approaching a line of trees bear left to a wall-corner, and follow the wall to a corner-stile into trees. Go straight through and Slaidburn appears ahead. Descend towards it, locating a stile back onto the road just short of the bridge over Croasdale Brook: cross to re-enter the village.

St Andrews, Slaidburn

19

3

EASINGTON FELL

START Slaidburn   Grid ref. SD 713523

DISTANCE 7½ miles

ORDNANCE SURVEY MAPS
1:50,000
Landranger 103 - Blackburn & Burnley
1:25,000
Outdoor Leisure 41 - Forest of Bowland & Ribblesdale

ACCESS Start from the village green, across the road from the large car park. Slaidburn is served by bus from Clitheroe, and infrequently from Settle. Newton is also served by the Clitheroe bus.

For a few notes on Slaidburn, please refer to page 15.

☐ *Leave by crossing the bridge and climb to the steep bend. Fifty yards beyond, take a gate on the right and bear right up the field. There are immediate views over the village to the wall of fells beyond; ahead is an early prospect of our fell for the day. **Pass a wood** to reach a gate at the far end, and advance along the wallside past a plantation. From a gate in the wall resume with a gentle descent to a road. Cross straight over and down the drive to Broadhead Farm, with its plethora of yapping dogs. Keeping left of the buildings, go round the back and, noting an improvised waymark for Skelshaw, leave things behind by crossing a farm bridge.*

A gate to the right leads to an enclosure which is crossed half-left to a gate in the fence above, before bearing right up the field to locate a stile in the top corner above the attractive Skelshaw Brook. Rise up the field, dropping from the brow into a small cluster of trees. An old gate give access to the messy enclosure before crossing the brook and rising to Skelshaw Farm. A track along the top side of the buildings runs out as the drive to join another drive. Turn sharply uphill to rise pleasantly through the fields to the aptly-named Fell Side. Look back to embrace an extensive panorama: in amongst the vastness of these eastern slopes - Totridge, Beatrix, Dunsop and Croasdale Fells - note also sleepy Newton nestling by the river Hodder.

Go straight ahead to tackle a gate at the back, then turn left to a gate onto the foot of the fell proper. A clear track, sometimes rutted and wet, heads away, quickly swinging up to the right with the contours of the hill. With Skelshaw Brook down to the left, the way rises increasingly pleasurably, still largely sunken until fading at a patch of bracken. Opt for one of the vague trods rising to the right: a reedy area is reached beneath a higher bracken tract, where the track re-establishes itself in the reeds. In amongst all this, also remember to look out from our fell to enjoy extensive Dales views from Fountains Fell along to Penyghent and Ingleborough.

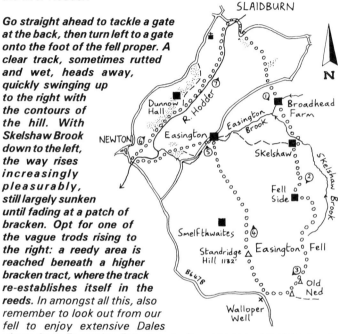

Emerging from reeds the track remains in magnificent condition, well defined throughout a leg-stretching tramp over Easington Fell. The infant beginnings of the brook are crossed emerging from a marshy hollow: later the way swings right up a gentle rake then runs on past a feeble cairn (Old Ned) to a sturdier pile at a junction. Ahead a working quarry is evident on the felltop: that, the mast above it and the appearance of a road cruelly shatter illusions of wilderness. Over to the left, as consolation, are the upper contours of Pendle Hill. *From the junction of green trackways continue on to meet the Clitheroe-Slaidburn road.* Just before this point a green *trod runs from a shooting butt to cross the grassy retaining wall of a former dam to meet the road a little higher, where spring water pours into stone troughs at Walloper Well, opposite. The drained reservoir served a waterwheel that worked a small lead smelting mill downstream.*

Return immediately to the moor, cross the tiny stream and - with no path - bear left, contouring around rough moorland in the company of telegraph poles. As these turn down to parallel the beck and the road, keep straight on over a little brook and up to reach a stone shooting butt. While one sunken way descends straight from it, just a few yards above it the upper one of three parallel sunken ways heads off: this drops to cross a tiny side-stream then leaves you free to ascend the rough slope to the prominent cairn on Standridge Hill just ahead. *This proves to be a broad felltop running north to Sadler Hill, with a pool in the saddle.*

Walloper Well

Leave by resuming in the same direction to a well-defined edge. *Here take in a great prospect: below, fields fall to the Hodder, which winds between Newton and Slaidburn, with the great wall of Bowland fells as backdrop. In the fields below is white walled Smelfthwaites Farm.* **Our way descends the bank to a kink in the wall, locating a stone stile alongside a collapsing ladder-stile. Don't descend to the farm but slant across to a barn in the far corner.**

From a gate on the near side of the barn, head down the field-side, from a stile at the bottom continuing down to another. Down another field-side, a gate is reached alongside a triangular wood, and a wall leads down to the farm buildings at Easington. *In this last field the prominent big house in view across the river is Dunnow Hall, passed on the final leg of the walk.* **Approaching Easington a track forms to cross a stream, becoming enclosed to emerge onto a narrow road.**

Go left for 150 yards and take a gate on the right. A large pasture is crossed diagonally - with the houses of Newton as guide - to a crumbling stile onto the bend of an old green road, now of use only to walkers. Advance along it, bridging the substantial Easington Brook. Just beyond is a brief enclosed spell, and the way narrows considerably to be squeezed alongside the Hodder's bank. Short-lived, this emerges into a field for the final yards to Newton Bridge. For refreshment or a potter round head up into the village - in its prominent location the inn cannot be missed: se WALK 4 for a little more on Newton.

Friends' Meeting House, Newton

Back at the bridge, take a gate in a gap-stile on the near side and head upstream. The path enjoys an opening spell by the wooded bank before a footbridge sends it along a field-side. A tiny slab footbridge and stile at the end see it on a longer field-side, narrowing as the river returns. The path, not shown as such on the map, enters the foot of a lovely wooded bank under the knoll of Great Dunnow. Emerging via an old iron kissing-gate into another large pasture, the austere Victorian pile of Dunnow Hall appears.

Advance to a vehicle track emerging from a river bridge, from where a permissive path heads upstream in glorious surrounds. The grassy bank of the Hodder is a real delight, even allowing for the interruption of a sewage works. An impressive limestone scar thrusts out of the wooded bank above, while Slaidburn's church soon appears, gathering its flock around it. **Back with the river beyond the deflection, we trace its bank all the way back to the village.** The big house of Whiteholme is well seen on the opposite bank. **Our way merges with a footpath from the church as it runs through a pocket wood to debouch onto the green.**

23

4

WHITEWELL

START Newton   Grid ref. SD 697504

DISTANCE 8½ miles

ORDNANCE SURVEY MAPS
1:50,000
Landranger 103 - Blackburn & Burnley
1:25,000
Outdoor Leisure 41 - Forest of Bowland & Ribblesdale

ACCESS   Start from the village centre. Newton is served by the
Clitheroe-Slaidburn bus. There is also parking space down by the
river across the bridge, while *bona fide* customers might be able
to use the pub car park, if they ask, and it is not too busy.
Alternative starts with parking space are Whitewell and Burholme
Bridge.

*Newton is a lovely, mellow stone village, dividing loyalties between
dark moors and the sparkling Hodder. Prominent near the river is
the Georgian Parkers Arms, a welcoming hostelry whose menu
caters for families. Across the road is the similarly attractive Hall,
while throughout the village are many delightful old buildings.*

☐ *Leave the village on the Dunsop Bridge/Trough road. Note, just
before the last house, the Friends' Meeting House (illustrated in
WALK 3) just up a back lane. Dated 1767, it ceased its original role
in 1988, and is now a private house.* **Verges assist with the opening
half-mile.** *This section enjoys views over the river to Hodder Bank
Fell, and beyond to the greater mass of Totridge.* **Just beyond a pair
of 'aqueduct' gates, and with a farm in sight ahead, take a stile on
the left. Slant across to another stile and maintain this line to a
corner at the end of a section of wall. Drop down to the river to find
a waiting suspension footbridge. Across it, bear right up to to join
a broad driveway.**

Turn right along the drive through typical parkland, and ignoring a branch left (our return route) continue down to cross stone arched Giddy Bridge. With a 'private' sign ahead - and the Victorian Knowlmere Manor sporting a rare collection of chimneys - **turn up the bank to a gate in a wall-cum-ditch.** The big house is well seen through the trees. **Rise to a stile in the fence above, then up to the brow of the field and cross a stile to the right of a barn. Rise to a prominent gateway in the wall on the skyline just above, between two contrasting plantations. This gives access to the great wastes of Hodder Bank Fell.** First, however, look back over Hodder country: Easington, Beatrix and Dunsop Fells, much rolling lower country, and on a clear day a fine array of Craven heights.

An unassuming path rises through the tussocky clumps of Hodder Bank Fell. Over to the left is the wooded top of Kitcham Hill, the summit of Birkett Fell. As height is gained, the great prow of Totridge breaks the skyline ahead. **A sunken way leads onto the brow, where some fainter moments ensue. The playful path wends an obvious way, however, through the saddle to angle left to a wall-corner. From the stile the path crosses to the right side of the wooded line of the broadening Fielding Clough. Immediately in better shape, it runs down the top of a bracken bank between beck and fence.** This remains a grand descent throughout its course, with super views of the valley to come, and Burholme Bridge appearing beneath the limestone skyline of Long Knots.

At the bottom a stile into the field finds another just below. Below that a gate gives access to Burholme Farm. Centuries ago this was a hamlet, and recent excavations have revealed much evidence of those busier times. *Cross a footbridge by a ford and follow the drive out to Burholme Bridge (illustrated in WALK 7)* enjoying the brief company of the Hodder. *Turn left on the road to Whitewell.* Caution is required on the narrower section: a riverside path down to Whitewell would be a real boon. Higher Whitewell Farm is passed before a wooded bank and a lovely river bend form a classic Bowland scene looking across to Totridge.

Cheek by jowl at Whitewell are inn and church - there is not a great deal else, but it's a charming spot. The little church of St Michael dates from 1818, on the site of a much earlier chapel. The Inn at Whitewell *is an old fashioned country hotel: pay extra for a peat fire in your room!* This was the former manor house, and incorporated in the present building are parts dating back over 500 years. Fishing is popular hereabouts, while a pack of hounds are kennelled within earshot. The inside of the place lives up to its attractive exterior, and welcoming rooms exude just the right sort of atmosphere. If you can afford to become ensconced, remember the return leg is a higher level crossing than the outward one.

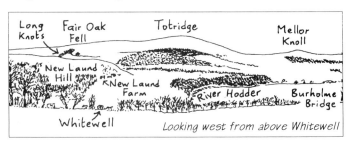

Looking west from above Whitewell

Leave by the minor road climbing from the green, bound for Clitheroe. Within yards a footpath sign points up a few steps to a rickety gate, from which rise to the house at Seed Hill. Cross its drive, and behind the house trace a line of trees climbing to a wall-corner at the top. At the gate look back over the valley: part of the panorama - which stretches from Parlick to Beatrix Fell - is depicted above. *From the gate an embanked green track heads away,* constructed to serve limestone quarries, some being visible ahead. *An early branch left for the nearest workings is ours, passing beneath the scars and by a fine limekiln to a gate onto a lane.*

26

From a gate opposite, a scruffy track heads up the field, but we keep above it to advance to a ladder-stile in the wall ahead. Down to the left is a small wood, while on the skyline is a dark plantation. Rise up the vast reedy pasture, past a clump of trees enshrouding the superb limestone shaft of Hell Hole Pot: though part-fenced, care is needed if approached. Whilst aware of the presence of limestone hereabouts, such a feature still looks out of place here instead of the flanks of, say, Ingleborough.

At the top a wall-stile, not too obvious, admits to the plantation, and a broad path heads away through the darkness. Daylight soon returns at the other end.

Hell Hole Pot

A fine prospect awaits, with Beatrix Fell to the left, Easington Fell ahead, and the Craven hills far across Ribblesdale. **From the stile cross the reedy field-top, edging left down to a gate. Through a slender plantation continue on a similar field-top to Crimpton Farm. Go straight through the yard as directed and out along its drive.**

Turn left along the road, a gentle rise passing Marl Hill Farm with its stand of weathered Scots Pine opposite, enjoying sweeping vistas. On the brow here a clear day will see Ingleborough looking very distant, directly ahead. **At a wooden cow byre in the field beyond the farm, turn through the gate and down the wall-side. Through a gate and down to the corner, a step-stile admits to a vast reedy pasture with Birkett Fell outspread ahead. Descend left of the bulk of the reeds - possibly locating a track of sorts - but then cross the brook as it becomes more assertive above an old sheepfold by the main brook - Birkett Brook.**

Somewhere here the Roman road from Ribchester to Over Burrow in the Lune Valley is crossed, if you find it you've done better than me. **Slanting down to Birkett Brook a solitary tree is a useful pointer, and a sunken way suddenly forms to lead down to it. Across the brook the way quickly reforms beyond the tree, and rises distinctly to arrive at a wall-corner. Take the ladder-stile over the wall,**

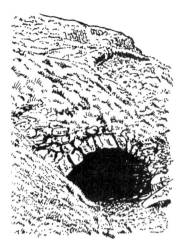

adjacent to the gateway. **Now descend towards the bottom corner of the large enclosure, with Higher Birkett Farm in view ahead. A track forms to ford a slabby beck at the bottom and rises up to the farm. Pass through the yard - noting an older central portion with mullioned windows - and out on its drive to Birkett Bridge.**

The limekiln above Whitewell

The drive runs out to meet the outward route just above Giddy Bridge. Turning right, this time remain on the drive throughout its course (a 200-yard section mid-way along is a permissive path, the public path returning to the suspension bridge then re-crossing the fields back to the drive!) **to join a back lane. Turn left, and 100 yards beyond the bridge take a stile on the left. Bear gently away from the road, over the brow to a stile by a gate at the far end. Now slant down to a more prominent stile to gain the riverbank. The Hodder is now followed upstream for the final yards.** *This makes a fine conclusion, with the hill of Great Dunnow prominent ahead and the Hodder as charming as ever.* **A slight deviation from the bank to a stile in a corner precedes the final yards to Newton Bridge. Re-cross to finish.**

The Parkers Arms, Newton

28

5

WHITENDALE

START Dunsop Bridge   Grid ref. SD 660500

DISTANCE 9 ½ miles

ORDNANCE SURVEY MAPS
1:50,000
Landranger 103 - Blackburn & Burnley
1:25,000
Outdoor Leisure 41 - Forest of Bowland & Ribblesdale

ACCESS   Start from the village green. There is a car park across the road. Dunsop Bridge is served by the Clitheroe-Slaidburn bus.

Though there is rather a lot of tarmac on this walk, it is all farm roads, not public roads, much with good verges, too.

Dunsop Bridge is a tiny Bowland village, under the influence of the Duchy of Lancaster estate and the water authority. Before starting out inspect the telephone box, the 100,000th public payphone installed by BT. A notice within advises that it marks the centre of Great Britain and 401 associated islands, having been calculated by the Ordnance Survey to a 10-figure grid reference. Town names adorn the windows, while outside, in a little rock garden, wooden posts mark points of the compass.

☐ ***Cross the bridge by the Post office to leave the green and follow the road up to the war memorial. Here branch right on the private road, passing the Forestry office.*** *Running through a field it reveals a fine surround of domed moorland heights, with Totridge over-shadowing Mellor Knoll back to the left, Staple Oak Fell just ahead, and Beatrix Fell further to the right. In between these latter two is our dark trough of the Dunsop, its walls lined by dark plantations.* ***Past a farm the road drops to the river at a footbridge. Continue*** *upstream, passing the isolated Bishops House and on between the trees. The plantations do not impinge down to the road, there being no feeling of claustrophobia. **Ahead, Middle Knoll appears to block the dale head, where it overlooks the meeting of the Brennand and Whitendale rivers.** These valleys were devastated by floods after a freak cloudburst in 1967. Approaching waterworks buildings, note the dry course of the old Brennand, moved for convenience.*

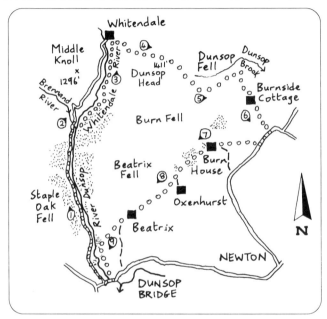

At the confluence our road crosses the Brennand. *Here the river Dunsop is born to a meagre two miles of existence before entering the Hodder at Dunsop Bridge.* ***Leave the road by crossing a second bridge, over the Whitendale, and taking the track upstream. Beneath a canopy of conifers, head on to the track's demise.*** *This section is particularly enjoyable, being deeply enclosed between steep slopes.* ***At an inflowing stream a path takes over, climbing towards one of two footbridges over a water pipeline. Crossing the stream below, the bridges are unlikely to be used. From the left bridge a path contours on the line of the pipe,*** *a smashing walk as Whitendale opens out: iron posts recall Blackburn Water Works.*

With the farm buildings ahead (a lovely oasis in its bowl of fells) the path makes for them, our way being through heather at the foot of the moorland flanks. At a field before the barns (the farmhouse sits alone, nearer the beck) the way runs above the wall to draw level with the barns. Here turn steeply right, on a track climbing directly up the moor. A big zigzag leads to a gate onto the moor proper, and the track resumes steeply. As the farm disappears from view on passing between shooting butts, a slight easing of the way sees a fork: keep straight on up, the clear path identifiable by marker posts and occasional cairns. Retrospective views increase as height is gained, Wolfhole Crag appearing across upper Whitendale.

Last view of Whitendale Farm

The climb continues for some time at a gentler pace, through black peat in the heather. Waymarks are largely superfluous on this generally good path. On the highest point, a near 360 degree prospect is revealed as views open out to north and east. Beyond the Bowland moors, Pendle Hill leads the eye to South Pennine heights, while Penyghent and Fountains Fell make a shapely Dales skyline. *A fork left towards the fence is ignored as the main path runs on towards a wall.*

Pass through the small gate into a contrastingly grassy tract of fell. Don't be tempted by stakes sending a path directly away. Instead, turn right with the wall for 150 yards, then bear gently away on a faint track. Beyond a small marsh a clear track unfolds, with the deep cut side-valley of Dunsop Brook below. The track runs around its head before descending the right-hand shoulder in fine style. Our track is part of a network of braided sunken ways, which enjoy a prospect over upper Hodder country to Stocks Reservoir backed by Gisburn Forest.

As a wall is neared, the sunken way swings back to the right to drop towards a wall: keep right on until the track's demise at a hidden gate. With the white-walled Burnside Cottage in view below, a green path runs down a reedy pasture towards it. On approaching it, cross the tiny stream to the wall and go through a gate. Two small enclosures lead down to a tiny bridge and gate onto the drive. Turn down it, and out through reedy pastures, crossing en-route the line of the Roman road from Ribchester to Over Burrow in the Lune Valley.

On joining a lane, turn right over a brow, with the long wall of Beatrix, Burn and Dunsop Fells to our right. *At the first house (Laythams) take a gate on the right, and head diagonally across the field,* re-crossing the line of the Roman road. *Aim for the prominent farm of Burn House, tucked under the fell. Over the brow descend by a fence to a track up to a barn, but cross straight over to a two-slab bridge. Continue to a fence-stile near the wall on the left, then advance a little further to a stile in the wall. Slant up the field to join the surfaced farm drive. Entering the yard, keep above all the buildings to remain on the drive past a couple of plantations to reach The Hey.*

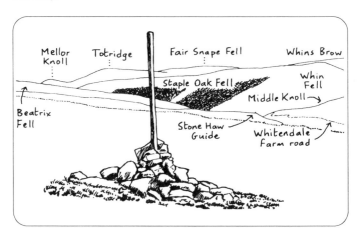

Looking south-west across the Dunsop Valley from the track to Dunsop Head, high above Whitendale

Beyond the house, the drive runs on to Oxenhurst. As it bears left before descending to it, leave it and keep straight on: the right of way goes through a gate just before the fence corner, and down the right side of the tiny stream and fence. A stile then leads into trees to approach Oxenhurst Clough, with grand views ahead to the Little Bowland area, and the limestone knolls of Long Knots prominent. *Drop down through the small plantation to the defile of Oxenhurst Clough. Up the wooded bank opposite, head away with a fence now on the right, and as it swings right, some way on, Beatrix Farm appears below.* Also in view now is Dunsop Bridge sheltering beneath Mellor Knoll and Totridge, with the Hodder winding away to its left. *Descend to the farm, join the drive and following it round to the right.* Two houses survive from what was once a busy hamlet.

Through a gateway just past the buildings, turn up into the field and head away with a line of telegraph poles. Passing a couple of sheep bields on the brow, drop down this vast pasture to a stile at the bottom. A path descends a wooded bank to the riverside. Turn downstream to a terrace of dwellings at Holme Head. The drive leads back, sometimes with the winding river, to emerge by the Post office.

Dunsop Bridge

33

6

BRENNAND VALLEY

START Dunsop Bridge   Grid ref. SD 660500

DISTANCE 8 miles

ORDNANCE SURVEY MAPS
1:50,000
Landranger 103 - Blackburn & Burnley
1:25,000
Outdoor Leisure 41 - Forest of Bowland & Ribblesdale

ACCESS Start from the village green. There is a car park across the road. Dunsop Bridge is served by the Clitheroe-Slaidburn bus.

Dunsop Bridge is a tiny Bowland village, which in the interests of space is described, along with its church, at the start of WALK 7.

◻ **Cross the bridge by the Post office and follow the road away past the war memorial. At a junction with the Lancaster road turn right for the Trough.** *The modern guidepost supplements a far more individual one dated 1739, with mileage for Slaidburn, Hornby, 'Clithero' and 'Lankster'. Embedded in the top, an iron post forlornly points to the 'Trough road'.* **On past the school and the Roman Catholic church, the open road is reached at a cattle-grid.**

Surrounds are now reminiscent of a Scottish glen. The bulky wall on the skyline to the left is Totridge. **Shortly, a drive goes down to a bridge over Langden Brook.** *Whilst the road with its verges is fine in itself, we have the option of a concessionary riverside path created by the water authority.* **Remain on the drive a short way after the bridge, but past the trees take a gate into the field on the right. A bridge crosses Hareden Brook to gain a stile accessing Langden Brook. Head upstream, initially flanked by a wall before an inviting, rough grassy sward leads to a substantial bridge. Cross it to a broad drive through pine trees, and turn right to return to the** *road. An inviting side-stream suggests a minor short-cut. The roadside route passes Smelt Mill Cottages, the base of the Bowland Pennine Mountain Rescue Team. Here a mill smelted lead that was mined a mile further up the road, which we shall shortly pass.*

Continuing, the road becomes briefly enclosed to pass through the complex at Sykes Farm. *This centuries-old settlement was once a vaccary farm and a sizeable farming hamlet: there are some 17th century datestones.* **Beyond, the road runs more freely through increasingly encroaching fellsides.** *This little side-valley leading through the Trough is Losterdale, and its beck is a tinkling delight when not under contract to the water authority.*

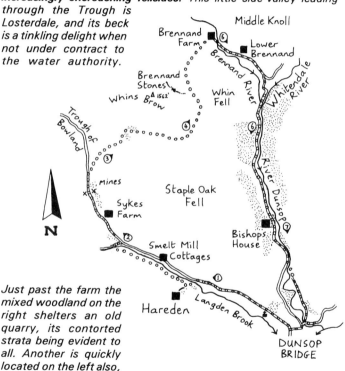

Just past the farm the mixed woodland on the right shelters an old quarry, its contorted strata being evident to all. Another is quickly located on the left also, above a well-preserved roadside limekiln. Here lead was won: only a small-scale operation, but a rare feature for Bowland. **Just after the road bridges the beck, Trough Barn is reached: this is a good time to leave as the road begins its haul to the Grey Stone of Trough, the traditional county boundary.**

Through the gate a distinct track climbs above a wooded bank, around a plantation and on to the scant remains of Trough House. Ahead is a broad amphitheatre below the skyline horseshoe of Whins Brow and Staple Oak Fell. **The track continues through an enclosed section beneath new plantings. At the end advance with the wall until it falls away, then aim along a path, sometimes a thin trod, slanting through rough pasture to a tall ladder-stile in the corner. Turn left up by the shaly ravine behind, a cairn and a stake confirming the route of the slim but distinct path as it breasts the level ground of the moortop.** *Here Whins Brow and Staple Oak Fell meet, and civilisation seems a comfortingly long way away. Sweeping landscapes increase as big views open out to the right, far beyond Bowland to Pendle Hill and the Pennine moors.*

The limekiln above Sykes

Joining a fence on the right the path runs on to a watershed fence junction. Ahead, seek out a distant Fountains Fell on the skyline. **Head straight on from the stile, soon swinging left to find ground suddenly falling away to reveal a cracking prospect of the Brennand Valley at our feet, immersed in sombre moorland. Brennand Farm, our objective, is directly below, with Low Brennand appearing to the right.** *Definitely a moment to halt and take stock! The low col behind the farm was the site of a bigger lead mining venture - this ore was also carried over Ouster Rake to the smelt mill.*

In winter conditions a little care is needed in negotiating the next stage, a rapid descent of the rake. *This bridleway on the map is today very much a footpath on the ground. Whilst on the map, the Brennand Stones just across to the left prove to be over-zealously drawn.* **The most enjoyable part is quickly over as we drop to a gate in a wall-corner. Beyond it a thin trod descends, then part-sunken**

reedy ways lead to a stile in a fence. Continue straight down a grassier pasture to the waiting farm. A couple of enclosures precede its yard, and beyond the house its surfaced drive heads off down-dale.

Whilst the return is largely surfaced road, it has the advantages of virtually no vehicles; many good verges; and grand surroundings. *A bridge over the Brennand river sends us to Low Brennand Farm. Rising away, a dark wall of conifers in the main valley awaits. A junction is quickly reached* with a long view down-valley: the left branch runs up Whitendale to similarly isolated Whitendale Farm. These valleys were devastated by floods after a freak cloudburst in 1967. After halting to look back to a lonely Brennand scene, *turn down to the right, the road leading unfailingly back to the village.*

At the confluence of Brennand and Whitendale rivers our road crosses the former. Here the river Dunsop is born to a meagre two miles of existence before entering the Hodder at Dunsop Bridge. Past some waterworks note the dry course of the old Brennand. From here our way is channelled too, by plantations on the lower flanks of Staple Oak and Beatrix Fells. *Our riverside road's enclosure is never claustrophobic, however, and soon more breathing space is found as the road runs on to the solitary Bishops House. An open half-mile beside the river leads to a footbridge. Either remain on the road to re-enter the village, or cross the bridge to a woodland path downstream to a terrace of dwellings at Holme Head. The drive leads back, sometimes with the winding river, to emerge by the Post office.*

*Middle Knoll from the Brennand
at its confluence*

7

UNDER TOTRIDGE

START Dunsop Bridge   Grid ref. SD 660500

DISTANCE 6½ miles

ORDNANCE SURVEY MAPS
1:50,000
Landranger 103 - Blackburn & Burnley
1:25,000
Outdoor Leisure 41 - Forest of Bowland & Ribblesdale

ACCESS Start from the village green. There is a car park across the road. Dunsop Bridge is served by the Clitheroe-Slaidburn bus.

Dunsop Bridge is a tiny Bowland village, under the influence of both the Duchy of Lancaster estate and the water authority. Before starting out, have a look at the telephone box, celebrated as the 100,000th public payphone installed by BT. A notice within advises that it marks the centre of Great Britain and 401 associated islands, having been calculated by the Ordnance Survey to a 10-figure grid reference. Town names adorn the windows, while outside, in a little rock garden, wooden posts mark points of the compass.

☐   **Cross the bridge by the Post office to leave the green and follow the road away past the war memorial. At a junction with the Lancaster road turn right, bound for the Trough.** *The modern guidepost serves only to supplement a far more individual one dated 1739, and inscribed with mileage for Slaidburn, Hornby, 'Clithero' and 'Lankster'. An old iron post embedded in the top forlornly points to the 'Trough road'.* **On past the primary school is the isolated Roman Catholic church of Our Lady and St. Hubert.** *Dating from 1864, and with some nice stained glass, it has links* *with the Towneley family. St. Hubert, incidentally, died in 727, and was a patron saint of hunters and protector against mad dogs. We shouldn't need his services on this walk.*

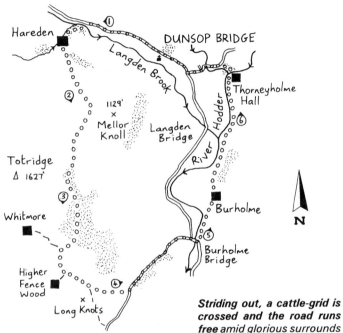

Striding out, a cattle-grid is crossed and the road runs free *amid glorious surrounds* reminiscent of a Scottish glen. The bulky wall of Totridge is prominent up to the left. Our walk, however, will cut back under its steep upper slopes and behind Mellor Knoll, in front of it. **Shortly a drive goes down to a bridge over Langden Brook. Cross it and follow along to the farming hamlet of Hareden. Cross the bridge on Hareden Brook to run along the characterful front of the farmhouse** - which dates back several centuries - **then quickly back over another bridge before an attractive white cottage. At once leave the track by a stile on the left to rise up the field,** pausing to look back over this sequestered scene. **Bear left to a stile and gate at the top corner to meet a track, which skirts the outside of a plantation before fading. Climb half-right up the steep pasture, eventually meeting a wall at the top. Go left with it and a green track forms to reach the top corner, and the end of the day's climbing.**

39

Up to the right is the seamed face of Totridge, while behind is an intimate prospect of the fair Trough of Bowland. **From the stile continue up a little further, then leave the track just before its zenith on a gently banked green way to the right. This flounders in badly drained ground: simply remain on the watershed.** *A final glance back offers the finest view into the heart of the Trough. Ahead, meanwhile, the whaleback of Longridge Fell is on parade to the left of the plantation.* **A ladder-stile also beckons ahead, the OS map being slightly out of step with the more obvious line of the path.**

A faint green path heads away, slanting down to the corner of a wood. *The crossing enjoys a wide prospect of the valley floor by which we shall return, with the Hodder displaying lazy ox-bows, and Pendle Hill upstanding amongst lesser heights.* **Beyond a stile and hand-gate the path drops towards a track, but cuts a corner by bearing right to join it at a sprightly beck crossing. The track contours above a scattered wood, an improving green way between an old wall and a fence. All too soon the plantation is reached.** *On entering, look back far to the north to discern the outline of Penyghent.* **The way through the dark regiments is foolproof, a broad path gently declining to the far end.**

Emerge with relief *to find Longridge still ahead and Fair Oak Fell's steep flanks immediately to our right.* **A green way heads off to meet a surfaced farm drive at a complex of hen huts. Go left, and**

Burholme Bridge, looking to Totridge

at a junction below, left again to head away from another farm. On the brow we are confronted by dark holes that are the remains of lead workings and quarrying amongst the limestone knolls. *As the drive swings right towards a cattle-grid, bear left down to a gate in the corner.* Before passing through, glance back to the left to note a big quarry hole incongruous in the otherwise green hillside.

Descend the large pasture, relishing views up the valley floor, with the Hodder snaking down from Dunsop Bridge: behind is Dunsop Valley, while distantly, Penyghent and Fountains Fell return. *A gate at the bottom sees us onto a back road, which leads down to a junction at Burholme Bridge.* Two irregular arches span the Hodder, a good foreground to grand scenery both up and down-stream.

Cross the bridge and turn on the drive to Burholme Farm. Go past the front of the house to a footbridge and ford just behind, then cross a couple of fields to gain the riverbank with Langden Holme Farm just across. From these fields look back to a skyline broken by those limestone knolls of Long Knots. *Upstream a rough pasture is entered via an old iron gate.* The gentle watersmeet of Langden Brook and the river is passed, with Langden Bridge marking the brook's final crossing. *Shortly, a big iron footbridge is reached,* erected in 1882 by Blackburn Corporation Waterworks to carry a pipeline to thirsty townsfolk. It is fronted by an antiquated turnstile which gives access to a better vantage point over the Hodder.

Resume up the bank to a stile, and on to an old kissing-gate, before a tree-lined pasture leads along to a farm drive at Thorneyholme. At one time owned by the Towneley family, the hall has been a nunnery and a hotel before its current role as a health farm. *The footpath is ushered round the outside of the house to its access bridge,* allowing us to see a second watersmeet as the river Dunsop is absorbed by the Hodder in delectable surrounds. *The bridge carries the drive, and thus our path, out to emerge back in the village opposite the car park.*

Old guidepost, Dunsop Bridge

8

FIENDSDALE

START Langden Intake   Grid ref. SD 632511

DISTANCE 10 miles

ORDNANCE SURVEY MAPS
1:50,000
Landranger 102 - Preston & Blackpool
1:25,000
Outdoor Leisure 41 - Forest of Bowland & Ribblesdale

ACCESS Start from a parking area at the beginning of Langden Intake water authority road, 2 miles west of Dunsop Bridge. • The section between Langden Castle and Fiendsdale Head is on water authority permissive paths: please take extra care during the bird nesting season: don't bring dogs.

An excursion into the Langden Valley seeks out deep recesses in the folds of the moors, linked by a high-level and invariably sometime marshy moorland trek.

❑ **From the gates head along the drive flanked by pines.** *Over to the right is Sykes Farm, last settlement this side of the Trough.* **At the waterworks house the drive bears round to the right, to end at the intake works.** *A sign on the gate including 'no guns' amongst its don'ts is guaranteed to raise a hollow laugh.* **Beyond the gate a rough track sets out into the lonely valley of Langden Brook. A spell by the flood plain is bettered as the track rises above a tiny wooded bank: at a fork keep left.**

Easy walking on a level terrace allows time to get acquainted with this lovely dale. Grand views throughout include the upper recesses of Fiendsdale appearing far ahead: part-way along we pass beneath a hardy oakwood. **In time a rise to a junction can be eschewed where a cairn indicates a footpath that maintains the** *contouring line. Just ahead, the roof of Langden Castle appears, and the path rejoins the track to descend to it.* Langden Castle is something of a let-down, being merely a shepherd's shelter: its construction, however, points to former use as a shooters' cabin.

This is the point to which the walk will return, after a circular trek round wilder country. Our initial objective is the side-valley of Bleadale (not to be confused with Bleasdale, to the south over the main watershed) the large valley coming in directly opposite. **From the front of the building, head away to ford first Langden Brook above its confluence with Bleadale Water, the latter probably then being the less easy of the two to cross. On its south bank a path forms, becoming increasingly clearer to penetrate this beautiful clough.**

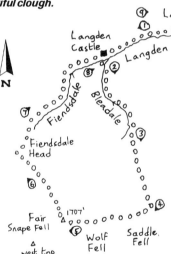

Tramped by generations of Bowland fellwanderers, this classic route has a long history of inter-valley use, suggesting it should in any case be a public path. **After a squeeze by the brook, the path runs between encroaching heathery walls, with the valley narrowing before re-opening on a wide, sweeping bend.**

Ahead, a side-stream falls towards us, though don't be tempted by the shooters' path rising very distinctly up the flank to the left. **Our way drops to cross the side-stream and on a further five level minutes to a confluence. Here twin stream merge, and though Brown Berry Clough, to the right, is certainly more pronounced, remain on the bank of the left branch.**

43

Continue upstream - still as Bleadale Water - with a final cluster of trees opposite. At once far more confined, scale the initially steep bank, and the slim path picks up above a few trees on our own side. The final section is a distinct trod through thick heather. Pause to look back over a fine array of interlocking spurs folding back down towards the moors beyond Langden Brook.

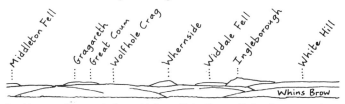

Looking to the north from high on Fair Snape Fell: the mountains of Three Peaks country overtop the Bowland moors

A confluence with a little fall is passed before finally gaining an amphitheatre where several tiny streamlets form **Bleadale Water.** *Here in this heathery bowl we might be anywhere, the view in these upper reaches being of only our enclosing moors.* **Emerging onto open moor with the path now run its course, forge due south up the gentle heather slope, navigation being little problem as the watershed is traced by a fence. Reaching it within ten minutes or so, the Saddle Fell/Wolf Fell access area is across it, while the permissive path shadows the fence.**

Turn right to commence a peaty traverse of the crest of Saddle Fell. A thin trod is of less help than the presence of the fence. *Distant views are now on offer, the sweeping moorland skyline of Bowland - with the crest of Totridge particularly prominent back along the ridge - is added to by Longridge Fell to the south, backed by the West Pennine Moors, and Pendle Hill further back to the left.*

The first of several numbered boundary stones is passed, the letters W and D supporting No. 31. **Soon an intervening fence is reached, and just down to the left a ladder-stile and access notice. A clear path runs back to the fence, and follows it over improving ground past No. 30 and up a gentle rise to the prone No. 29 at a fence corner.** *Over to the left, the rounded top of Parlick can be discerned.* **At the next fence corner we reach Fair Snape Fell. A further collection of stile, notice, and stone No. 28 mark the summit of the walk, though the highest point is the cairn just to the right.** *This stands at 1707ft, though its lower top at 1673ft across the marshy plateau is more often visited (see WALKS 10 and 11).*

A step-stile gives access to the summit cairn, and it is this fence we follow down to the north-west, a long, easy descent to Fiendsdale Head. The first section is entirely delightful on short-cropped turf between peaty knolls. Enjoy it, for soon moist ground takes over for the remainder of the way down to the saddle. Across Fiendsdale Head rise the Bleasdale grouse moors, bereft of footpaths. At a padlocked gate look back to the shapelier edge of Fair Snape, and across Bleasdale to the colourful crest of diminutive Beacon Fell. *Beyond the gate a slight rise leads to a stile and notice where we leave the access area for the public footpath just prior to a fence corner. If still on the south side, cross the stile and head north on an initially messy path with the fence parallel to the left.*

Within a minute the way improves, a peaty channel leading the path to easier ground. The head of Fiendsdale quickly forms, and a solid path takes over in the heather. This remains a brilliant path, soon visible some way hence as it contours around heathery flanks. On this leg the secretive atmosphere of Bleadale is traded for a wide open promenade. *The return to the valley floor comes suddenly in a rapid descent of Fiendsdale Nab. The dale is gained at the confluence of Langden Brook and Fiendsdale Water, a grand spot.*

Only the former brook is crossed, which should be easy if Bleadale Water was managed earlier in the walk. While the valley floor is dead flat, the path gains a modest bank and runs on to return to Langden Castle, merging into the shooters' track for the final yards. The presence of several sections of boardwalk testify to usage of the path, though it is surely insufficient to merit such over-the-top actions out here: indeed, the marshy sections they bridge are no worse than many others encountered by the paths. *All that remains is to retrace steps back to the start, a wholly pleasurable prospect.*

Langden Castle

45

9

LITTLE BOWLAND

START Chipping   Grid ref. SD 622432

DISTANCE 8½ miles

ORDNANCE SURVEY MAPS
1:50,000
Landranger 102 - Preston & Blackpool **or**
            103 - Blackburn & Burnley
1:25,000
Outdoor Leisure 41 - Forest of Bowland & Ribblesdale

ACCESS   Start from the village centre, by the church and the *Sun Inn*. There are two car parks on the Garstang road. Chipping is served by the Clitheroe-Longridge bus, and also by a once a week direct service from Clitheroe.

Chipping is an attractive stone built village, whose origins pre-date its emergence as a market town in 1203. Features of interest, including three pubs, are all near the junction of the two main streets. Worth seeing is a former school, endowed by cloth merchant John Brabin in 1683. It sports mullioned windows, and forms a tidy group with the adjacent almshouses. St Bartholomew's church dates from the 16th century, but was restored in Victorian times: great semi-circular steps from the main street are a novel feature. A cornmill has been converted to a restaurant, its wheel restored and visible from the road bridge on Chipping Brook. Wolfen Mill dairy produces Lancashire cheeses of the finest quality.

☐ *Leave by a side-road heading away between church and cafe. At a junction fork right, descending by the celebrated chair factory. Climb past it to the lovely setting of the millpond that once provided its power. Part-way along, turn off at a stile by a drive and head up the right side of the field.* Ahead, the cone of Parlick thrusts itself forward, while looking back, Longridge Fell forms a long skyline *over the village, with Pendle Hill set further back. **Keep straight on at the top:** ahead now is a great cirque of fells. **From a stile at the end, advance across a large field, bearing left to the edge of the bank of Dobson's Brook.***

A little further, a sunken way sends us off to contour around the bank to a stile part-way down. From it a thin path runs on to enter trees, and reaches a footbridge over the right arm of a confluence. Climb the field behind to the left of the house at Windy Hills, and turn right into the yard. Leave the drive up the far side of the barn, where a green track climbs the field-side. Though petering out at the top, it shows the way up through several stiles. Stay with the fence until just before a brow: here a waymark sends us off to the left, crossing this field and the next to join the farm road to Burnslack.

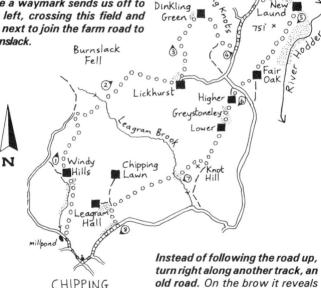

Instead of following the road up, turn right along another track, an old road. On the brow it reveals a good view out to the twosome of Pendle Hill and Longridge Fell, Ribble Valley's finest, while Burnslack and Fair Oak Fells form a great wall above us. *The track enters rough pasture to ford Leagram Brook.* At the far end we are greeted by a fine view of the ridge of Long Knots, the brink of limestone country. A long descent through a reedy enclosure leads to the farming hamlet of Lickhurst.*

Without entering the complex, go left down the drive (This offers a short-cut to Higher Greystoneley). Descend towards the bridge, but take a footbridge before it, at a confluence. Climb the field to a stile and up again, left of a small quarry, and a faint track curves round to a stile by a gate. Now bear left around the field-edge, with Dinkling Green appearing ahead. Remain on the boundary, passing a small pool and turning sharp right to advance towards the farm. Nearer, a track forms, going through a gate and running beneath a small plantation to enter the farmyard. Dinkling Green is a settlement of some age, having once been a much busier hamlet.*

Go straight ahead to leave by its drive. This curves round to the right under the limestone ridge of Long Knots. Part-way on, as the slope abates, take a gate on the left (benchmark on gatepost) and slant right to pick up a green way rising back up the slope. This is a grand spot, looking back to the high moorland wall of Fair Oak Fell. *Continue over the brow, where it re-appears to slant down to a gate. Head left along the lane,* to be greeted on the brow by a glorious prospect of the Hodder Valley running to Dunsop Bridge.

Gently descending, pass a farm road to the left, then leave the road at a gate beneath a quarry scar up to the right. Contour round beneath the big knoll of New Laund Hill, crossing to a gate in a fence corner. Continue away along the field top. Do this slowly to savour the prospect of Hodder country, some of which is depicted below.

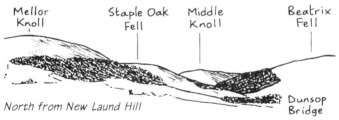

Mellor Knoll   Staple Oak Fell   Middle Knoll   Beatrix Fell

North from New Laund Hill   Dunsop Bridge

Part-way down, cross the fence to descend to a drive. Turn right into New Laund farmyard. A forest keepers' house once existed here. On New Laund's slopes, the 65ft long cave of Fairy Holes has revealed animal bones and an Early Bronze age urn. *Before reaching the house turn up to a gate between barns, a rough track climbs away. This fades, but points the way to the field top, beneath the steeper drop of New Laund Hill. Through a gateway,* acclaim a super revelation. Ahead, the Whitewell Gorge ushers the Hodder through rich woodland backed by Longridge Fell. Behind is a final up-dale prospect, and below is a cameo of Whitewell (WALK 4).

48

Don't rise too far with the track, but drop down to a ladder-stile visible ahead. In view beyond is the farmstead of Fair Oak, and a track forms to runs along the field-side to it. Just past the farmhouse, leave the drive by going right to an old barn before a large modern one. The old barn is known locally as the Gunnary, it bears a 1720 datestone and sports a whole range of slit windows. *From a gate to its left cross the field, bearing right of a farm visible ahead. A stile in the fence on the right at the end leads to two more, each side of a road. The second sends us straight across the field to Higher Greystoneley, joining its drive to enter the yard.*

Keep straight on, the drive then running down through woodland. New short paths and a tiny access area have been created here as part of the Countryside Stewardship scheme: a path to the left gives an alternative route to Knot Hill, if so desired. *The track descends to a ford and footbridge in the wood, then climbs to Lower Greystoneley. Again forge straight on, its drive running to a cattle-grid and barn in front of the broken skyline of Knot Hill. Turn up to the right here, a green track running between a pond and a limekiln to the edge of a substantial old quarry. At the end of the quarry, bear away from the line of trees to locate a stile in the fence ahead. From it bear left down the wooded bank, a grassy rake descending to a footbridge for a second crossing of Leagram Brook.*

Go upstream a short way to be deflected left with a fence up into a field. Now march straight along with a fence on the right, enjoying the moorland skyline above. When the fence ends, keep straight on through the parkland of Leagram Hall to join the drive. Leagram Hall is on the site of a lodge in this former deer park, while during the 16th century, this was a refuge for priests. *Follow this drive down to the road and turn right. Chipping church tower is a magnet for the final steps. Turn right in the village, passing the old watermill.*

The old watermill, Chipping

10

CHIPPING FELLS

START Chipping   Grid ref. SD 622432

DISTANCE 7½ miles

ORDNANCE SURVEY MAPS
1:50,000
Landranger 102 - Preston & Blackpool
1:25,000
Outdoor Leisure 41 - Forest of Bowland & Ribblesdale

ACCESS Start from the village centre, by the church and the
Sun Inn. There are two car parks on the Garstang road. Chipping
is served by the Clitheroe-Longridge bus, and also by a once a
week direct service from Clitheroe. •ACCESS AREA: A section
of this walk between Saddle Fell and Parlick is within the Saddle/
Wolf/Fair Snape Fells access area. This is closed on a number of
days during the grouse shooting season (not Sundays) and also
at times of high fire risk. Most important restrictions is 'no dogs'.
If in doubt, enquire with the Countryside Service, details on
page 110.

*Chipping is an attractive stone built village, whose origins pre-date
its emergence as a market town in 1203. Features of interest,
including three pubs, are all near the junction of the two main
streets. Worth seeing is a former school, endowed by cloth
merchant John Brabin in 1683. It sports mullioned windows, and
forms a tidy group with the adjacent almshouses.*

*St Bartholomew's church dates from the 16th century, but was
restored in Victorian times: great semi-circular steps from the main
street are a novel feature. A cornmill has been converted to a
restaurant, its wheel restored and visible from the road bridge on
Chipping Brook. Wolfen Mill dairy produces Lancashire cheeses of
the finest quality.*

□ *Leave by a side-road heading away between church and cafe. At a junction fork right, descending by the celebrated chair factory. Climb past it to the lovely setting of the millpond that once provided its power. Part-way along it turn off at a stile by a drive, and head up the right side of the field.* Already, Parlick thrusts itself forward in readiness. Looking back, Longridge Fell forms a long skyline over the village, with Pendle Hill set further back. *Keep straight on at the top: ahead now is the great cirque of fells that is to be ours. From a stile at the end, advance across a large field, bearing left to the edge of the bank of Dobson's Brook.*

A little further, a sunken way sends us off to contour around the bank to a stile part-way down. From it a thin path runs on to enter trees and reach a footbridge over the right arm of a confluence. Climb the field behind to the left of the house at Windy Hills, and follow its rough drive over Dobson's Brook and up onto a road noting, just before the road, an attractive tiny pond. Cross straight over and up the drive to the aptly-named Saddle End Farm. The cone of Parlick now dominates the scene in grand style.

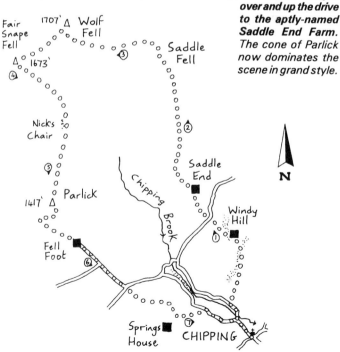

51

Rise into the yard, and directly up a grassy track climbing away. This runs on through a couple of enclosures, then rises as a braided way to a ladder-stile and access notice - and the fell proper. The good track continues, working a leisurely way up Saddle Fell: as the ways braid again, cairns suggest the middle one, though any is worthy. Looking back, Pendle and Longridge front a massive line of South and West Pennines, while Parlick starts to lose a little dominance. A prominent cairn with a stake precedes arrival at a ruin, as grassiness gives way to rougher ground including heather.

Parlick from
Saddle Fell

Nearing a fence rising with the head of the brook on the left, remain on the track which peters out just as a stile in the fence is seen. Crossing to Wolf Fell, a thin but clear path heads away. Before going far, however, turn to look back over a moorland foreground to a magnificent prospect of Three Peaks country.

The path runs on delightfully through heather, entirely free of the peatiness that bogs down the watershed fence up to the right. A glimpse of Parlick reveals only its upper reaches now, certainly not exciting at the moment. *Marked by occasional cairns the path expires on reaching a fence: turn right the few yards to the fence junction on Fair Snape's true summit. Here are ladder-stile, access notice and numbered War Department boundary stone* (the area was a training ground during the second world war). *A step-stile on the right invites a short detour to the waiting cairn, at 1707ft the summit of the walk.* The prospect is outstanding - see also WALK 8. Three Peaks country returns, joined by Morecambe Bay and the Lakeland Fells beyond a sprawl of Bowland.

Back at the fence-corner, either head south with the fence for a while, or in clear weather aim directly for the waiting cairns on Fair Snape's more popular western top, at 1673ft. This is certainly a place to linger, where two cairns and an OS column play second fiddle to an oft-appreciated stone shelter. Paddy's Pole, as marked on maps, is currently not embedded in the cairn where it belongs.

Leave by striking south-east for Parlick, its domed peak a positive magnet as it protrudes out into the green pastures from the mass of fells to which it belongs. *A delightful, short-cropped path runs eagerly through thin heather to regain the descending ridge.* The fields and farms of Bleasdale are encircled far below: beyond this neatly packaged farmland, the island-like Beacon Fell seems profoundly insignificant.

At the wall continue down to the waiting saddle, passing rashes of stones on the slopes where Nick's Chair sits flat-topped beyond most of them (illustrated in WALK 11). *At a cluster of stiles and an access notice, one can circumvent Parlick's summit by taking the track curving round to the left. More inviting, however, is the prospect of the short pull by the fence to gain the summit at 1417ft.* In truth this is an ordinary top, but its situation is not. The panorama from the great pile of stones is outstanding. Anti-clockwise we have the West Pennine Moors, the South Pennines, Longridge Fell, Pendle Hill, Easington Fell and round via Saddle Fell to the Bleasdale Moors. Looking back, Fair Snape's west top is now magnificent.

Easington Fell   Pendle Hill   Longridge Fell

Parlick's summit cairn, looking east

Leave by the only path, heading south-east to quickly encounter steep ground. Fell Foot Farm waits directly below, identified by a line of parked cars. Parlick (Parlick Pike is its rarely used Sunday name) is a haunt of hang-gliders, and if in evidence they add further *colour to the scene. As Parlick is naturally popular with 'ordinary' visitors too, the path up its steep flank is becoming rather worn.* **On encountering the traversing path, take advantage of its easy gradients and turn down to the right on one of its sunken ways, thence doubling back to the base of the fell.** *This not only prevents erosion, it makes a far more civilised descent anyway.*

At Fell Foot head down the lane. At a junction keeps straight on to a T-junction with Fish House Lane. *A quiet road walk can be enjoyed by going left, descent past the wooded clough of Chipping Brook being delightful with bluebells in bloom. Otherwise,* **cross straight over to a stile, and follow a crumbling wall away.** *The prospect back to our day's fells remains as good as ever, though not for long now.*

The old wall curves down Lingey Hill to be replaced by a few trees and a tiny beck. At a fence, the old way is impassable, and a stile in the fence ahead sees us down the field-side outside the morass. Approaching a barn, cross the beck to a wall-stile, and rise to a part-hidden stile by a kink in the fence above. Head directly away from this - with Springs House over to the right - to a stile onto its drive. Turn left to join a lane, and follow this down into the village.

Brabin's School, Chipping

┌─────────────────────────────────────┐
│   ⟨ **11** ⟩   │
│   │
│   # BLEASDALE FELLS   │
└─────────────────────────────────────┘

START Beacon Fell   Grid ref. SD 573427

DISTANCE 10 miles

ORDNANCE SURVEY MAPS
1:50,000
Landranger 102 - Preston & Blackpool
1:25,000
Outdoor Leisure 41 - Forest of Bowland & Ribblesdale

ACCESS   Start from the Quarry car park at the eastern end of
Beacon Fell Country Park. This involves descent and re-ascent
at the start and finish of the walk, but in the absence of parking
facilities in Bleasdale there is little alternative: compensation is
found in the opportunity to appraise the magnificent moorland
route in advance. Anyone getting a lift or arriving by bicycle
could best start at Bleasdale Post office. Beacon Fell is served
by Summer Sunday/BH Monday bus links with Chipping, Slaidburn
and beyond.

•ACCESS AREA: A section of this walk between Blindhurst and
Fiendsdale Head is within the Fair Snape Fell access area. This
is closed on a number of days during the grouse shooting season
(not Sundays) and also at times of high fire risk. Most important
restrictions is 'no dogs'. If in doubt, enquire with the Countryside Service, details on page 110.

*Beacon Fell was opened in 1970 as Lancashire's first country park,
comprising 185 acres of moorland and woodland. To Lancashire
folk it is a much valued and well used amenity. Various short walks
are laid out, and whilst they offer scope for exploring the 'park', it
is, in itself, a little small to plan a decent walk within its confines.
Further around the park a new visitor centre was opened in 1995,
providing information, displays, a shop, refreshments and toilets.*

□ *Leave the car park and return to the road, leaving the country park at once by the road heading east, down from the fell. Within yards leave this too by a stile on the left, and cross to the brow of the field before slanting right down to a fence corner.* From this field survey a magnificent prospect of Bleasdale country, backed by the great fells of Parlick and Fair Snape - ours for the taking. Also in view to the right are Easington Fell, Pendle Hill and Longridge Fell.

At the fence corner a track is joined to go down an old hollowed way. As it swings right for Wood Acre Farm, take a stile in front and continue down one more field-side. At the bottom corner note the stile to which we'll return at the end of the walk, but for now turn right along the bottom of the field to approach the farm.

A stile just before it keeps us out of its confines, advancing on to a gate to follow its drive out onto a lane. Go right as far as Watery Gate Farm, past which take a gate on the left just before a line of trees. Double back a little to trace a sunken pathway away with a fence. From a stile at the far end bear right over the brow, and cross towards Lower Core Farm. A gate in front admits onto a lane. Go left a good 100 yards and turn up the drive to Blindhurst.

Map labels:

Fiendsdale Head

Bleasdale Moors

N

Hazelhurst

Holme House

Admarsh Barn Farm

Vicarage Farm

Bleasdale *Circle

Bleasdale

Fair Snape Fell
1707'
1673'

Wolf Fell

Nick's Chair

Parlick
1417'

Blindhurst

Higher Brock Mill

Lower Core

Watery Gate

Quarry Car Park

Wood Acres

872'
Beacon Fell

Now we're really on the slopes of Parlick, which waits patiently and invitingly above. Entering the yard at Blindhurst, note the attractive front of the white walled house, with 1731 datestone and mullioned and transomed windows.

56

Pass right of the house into an enclosure, but instead of following the track away, turn up the wall-side to a corner. Just along - as a fence takes over - a green way slants up the field. This quickly levels out and crosses to a tiny brook, beyond which slant up to a stile onto the foot of the fell proper. Here a notice confirms arrival in the access area. Bear left up the grassy fellside to a fence, following it up to a corner. Here a track comes out of the field, and begins a zigzag climb up Parlick's steep contours. *Contrast the dry grassiness of our fell with the dark, heathery Bleasdale Moors across to the left. Finest of the open views is across to Fair Snape Fell.* **Approaching a crumbled wall, slant to the fence on the right. This leads up, soon easing out to attain the summit at 1417ft.**

In truth this is an ordinary top, but its situation is not: hang-gliders also find the place to their liking. The panorama from the great pile of stones is outstanding (see also WALK 10). Anti-clockwise we have the West Pennine Moors, the South Pennines, Longridge Fell, Pendle Hill, Easington Fell and round via Saddle Fell to the Bleasdale Moors. Looking back, Fair Snape's west top is now quite a magnet.

Our way resumes along the fence, dropping to a saddle where Nick's Chair sits flat-topped just over the edge. Old sunken ways ascend above the steep flank's rashes of stones. As the shoulder broadens the clear path swings left to leave the wall, and a delightful, short-cropped path curves through the thin heather to the waiting furniture on Fair Snape. *En route we encircle the green floor of Bleasdale. Its scattered farms are backed by the insignificant looking island of Beacon Fell.*

Fair Snape Fell from Nick's Chair

On Fair Snape, cairns and an OS column play support to a shelter. Paddy's Pole, marked on maps, is currently not embedded in the cairn where it should be. At 1673ft, this may only be the fell's western top, but it is the point to which all ramblers aspire. Far to the north, beyond miles of moorland, the Three Peaks are in view.

In poor visibility one can always turn back, having completed the best walking and the two best tops. **Otherwise, locate a cairn to the north-east marking the true summit, and head for it either directly or by first crossing to the fence. Either way, peaty terrain will be encountered. At a fence corner, ladder-stile, access notice and War Department boundary stone (see WALK 8) are reached just short of the cairn at 1707ft, accessed by a step-stile.** The outstanding prospect now includes Morecambe Bay and the Lakeland Fells beyond a sea of Bowland moors.

This fence leads north-west, a long, easy descent to Fiendsdale Head. The first section is entirely delightful on short-cropped turf between peaty knolls. Enjoy it, soon moister ground takes over. Across Fiendsdale Head rise the Bleasdale grouse moors. At a gate look back to the shapely edge of Fair Snape, and across Bleasdale to the crest of diminutive Beacon Fell. **Beyond the gate is a slight rise to a stile and access notice. Back on a public path, turn left, an initially peaty crossing to begin a return to the valley. This quickly dries into a stony path slanting down the fell,** Fair Snape increasing in grandeur with every step. **Suddenly the path transforms into a smooth green rake, a revelation.** Over to the left, Parlick reveals itself from behind Fair Snape. **At an access notice at the bottom, go forward with the wall until reaching a stile in it.**

Here turn down the field to cross a drive between Holme House and Hazelhurst. Though there is a stile directly below, the right of way officially goes right along the drive a short way before turning down to another stile before crossing to the field-side. Beyond a corner-stile, two wooden footbridges are crossed before a track runs along to Admarsh Barn Farm. The path goes left of all buildings to emerge onto the drive. This leads out, now surfaced, to Vicarage Farm. Over to the left, sequestered in trees, is the Bleasdale stone circle.

Bleasdale stone circle

The circle, on private land, is the subject of a management agreement with the county council. It may be visited by seeking permission at the school, further down the road past the church. If closed, try Bleasdale estate office, Bleasdale Tower: some initiative required here! Access to the circle is by leaving the road opposite Vicarage Farm drive, the previous and more logically sited place to enquire. Past the immediate trees, the route crosses a couple of fields bound for the unmistakable clump enclosing the circle. A stile admits to the hidden confines. Around 3000 years old, the circle dates from the Bronze age, yet was only discovered a century ago by a local farmer. A ditch 150ft in diameter encircles the burial mound, in which two cremations were found in collared urns. Small concrete pillars have replaced the original 11 posts that surrounded it, now housed in the Harris Museum at Preston.

Back at Vicarage Farm, head out on the drive to reach the church. St Eadmors dates from 1835, and was restored later that century. The first chapel stood here in 1637. The dedication is unique: Eadmer was biographer of several saints, including Anselm and Wilfred. He died in 1124, still a simple monk. **Back on the road go on past the school and village hall to emerge onto the road at Higher Brock Mill.** Just to the left is Bleasdale Post office and cafe. Originally a smithy, it is now a very tempting refreshment halt.

Go past the shop and (just over the brook) Higher Brock Mill itself, and head up the road. If seeking to explore more of Beacon Fell on returning, one can opt for the conclusion used in WALK 12. Otherwise, **follow the road up to a T-junction at Wickins Lane End. Go left for a couple of minutes to the former Dog & Partridge, opposite which leave the road by a bridge. Up through a small enclosure head along the field-sides, through a gateway to a broad gap-stile at the end. Head up to the top of the strip plantation opposite, where a stile crosses the fence. Resume up to the stile we didn't cross near the start of the walk, and retrace opening steps back to the car park.**

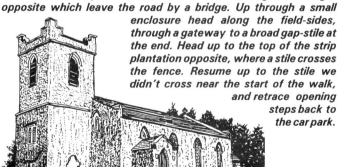

St. Eadmers
Bleasdale

12

RIVER BROCK

START Beacon Fell Country Park   Grid ref. SD 564426

DISTANCE 6½ miles

ORDNANCE SURVEY MAPS
1:50,000
Landranger 103 - Preston & Blackpool
1:25,000
Outdoor Leisure 41 - Forest of Bowland & Ribblesdale

ACCESS Start from the Bowland visitor centre at Beacon Fell Country Park, formerly the Fell House Information Centre. There is ample car parking available. Summer Sunday/BH Monday bus links with Chipping, Slaidburn and beyond.

Beacon Fell was opened in 1970 as Lancashire's first country park, comprising 185 acres of moorland and woodland. To Lancashire folk it is a much valued and well used amenity. The new visitor centre provides information, displays, a shop, refreshments and toilets. The original Fell House was a farmhouse, demolished in 1939. Various short walks are laid out, and whilst they offer scope for exploring the fell, it is too small to plan a decent walk within its confines. The principal feature of this walk is the river Brock, which offers a rare opportunity for an extended riverside ramble.

☐ *Two footpaths leave the car park, one in the centre, one to the right, where the car park joins the road. Take the right-hand one where a short track runs by the trees to a gate/stile into a field.* An immediately grand prospect reveals sweeping views of the Ribble estuary and surrounding plains. *Go down the left side of the field, outside the trees, passing a couple of stiles to reach a ladder-stile in the bottom corner. Continue down through a belt of trees to a private-looking gate marked 'Salisbury'. A little gem of a path runs down a stream-side to the white-walled house, and out along its drive.*

Turn left along the road, and bear right to pass a dam and Eccles Moss Farm, with its striking frontage. At the next junction keep right, passing further architectural interest in the form of Higher Stannalee Cottage with its thatched roof.
Keep on past one or two more dwellings to a sharp bend at another white house, then double back sharply on a path shrouded in greenery. It descends a hollowed way - a fine introduction to the Brock far below - *to the environs of the river at Brock Bottom.*

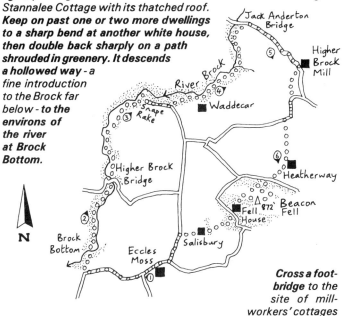

Cross a foot-bridge to the site of mill-workers' cottages just down to the left, and one of four mills the Brock once served: all succumbed long ago to steam powered mills that appeared on the plain below. *Head upstream on what has been dubbed the Brock Valley Nature Trail. This super walk -* understandably popular at weekends - *has few equals as it runs up to the Brock car park and picnic area at Higher Brock Bridge.* The car park is a minor culture shock, gained suddenly after the woodland surrounds.

Cross the bridge and turn upstream, below the house dubbed Brock Mill. A field is crossed to cut a bend of the river before the path clings tightly to its bank until approaching an aqueduct with a weir beneath. Before reaching the aqueduct, cut across to the end of its embankment to find a barn-like building below. Go to its right to locate the path continuing along the foot of the wooded bank. At the end the wooded riverbank resumes for a grand walk to the footbridge at Snape Rake. This historic ford was on a road used by the Romans.

Without crossing, double back sharply up the hollowed way, climbing steeply to a dead-end road. Why this should be surfaced, simply to end here, is anyone's guess. With Beacon Fell now prominent, directly ahead, those keen for an early finish can remain on Snape Rake Lane to a road junction and thence climb the hill to be finished within a half-hour. Otherwise, *advance along it just as far as the end of the wood on the left, re-entering at the last moment on a broad path slanting back down. As it doubles sharply back left, keep straight on over a tiny stream to a fence corner. Continue along the field-bottom, pick up a track descending from Waddecar.* Scattered cabins hereabouts are part of the county scout campsite, often with further evidence in the form of tents on the bank.

Eccles Moss Farm

Continuing, a footpath leaves the track to cling to the riverbank, and at the end of the trees runs through a couple of fields to a footbridge. This last section offers open views, with Fair Snape Fell filling the frame ahead. The bridge spans a side-stream as it enters the Brock. *Cross and resume with the Brock, quickly deflected up a gorse bank to a pair of stiles. The upper one takes the right of way along the outside of the wood, while the well-used left-hand one enters the trees for a super path to run along the top.* Here the best of both worlds is experienced in the transition from river to fell scenery: the Brock chuckles through the trees, while above is a prospect of the Bleasdale Fells, Fair Snape and Parlick. *At the end the path winds round,* above banks rich with bluebells in May, *to emerge onto a road, with Jack Anderton Bridge down to the left.*

Finally taking our leave of the Brock, turn right along the road - enjoying fell views that remain to the end - *for ten short minutes to Bleasdale Post office at Higher Brock Mill.* This former smithy boasts a cafe, tempting a halt for the delights of Lancashire ice cream and the like, a real surprise in this quiet corner.

Continue a few yards up the road, then take a flight of steps to follow a fence away. This rises through fields to emerge onto another lane at Wickens Barn. Throughout this return, Beacon Fell is entirely upstaged by the outstanding retrospect of the Bleasdale cirque. *Turn right, and leave at the first opportunity by a farm drive rising away. This runs to a fork: go straight ahead up the drive towards the big house at Heatherways, but then keep straight up to a gate directly ahead. Rise up near a fence and then slant gently right to locate a stile in a fence across the top. A thin path runs up to the road encircling Beacon Fell.*

Go right a few yards then take a potentially muddy path slanting through the plantation. Emerging onto a hard forest road, turn back to the left (being wary of bikes) *until it starts to descend. Here branch right for a few yards along a path before a stone-surfaced path doubles back up to the right. This rises to the waiting Ordnance column (S4701) crowning Beacon Fell at the modest height of 872 feet.* Affixed to it are a plaque and a view indicator. Some of its features are distinctly under-represented thanks to the growth of trees to south and east, though everything we want to see is readily on display. Not surprisingly the fell is named from its former role, as a beacon site for perhaps 1000 years: it was part of the chain that warned of the Armada's approach in 1588.

While the main path head s into the trees, savour the final fell views by heading west on a moorland path outside the trees. Shortly the path that brought us back onto the fell comes in from the right, and following it into the trees it makes a short descent to the start.

Beacon Fell, looking to Fair Snape Fell and Parlick

13

NICKY NOOK

START Scorton   Grid ref. SD 504503

DISTANCE 8 miles

ORDNANCE SURVEY MAPS
1:50,000
Landranger 102 - Preston & Blackpool
1:25,000
Outdoor Leisure 41 - Forest of Bowland & Ribblesdale

ACCESS Start from the Scorton picnic site, one mile north of
the village alongside the motorway. Scorton is served by bus
from Garstang.

*The environs of Scorton prove to be Bowland's modest answer to
the Lake District, and reveal a fascinating range of surroundings.*

◻ *Return to the road and cross straight over, where a footpath
sign points the way down a track parallel to the river Wyre. On
crossing a tiny stream, our way parts company by bearing gently
left across the field. Shortly a small watercourse comes in to lead
through the fields, being joined by Park Brook before emerging onto
a road just short of Scorton.*

*Turn right into the village centre, and at the staggered crossroads
turn up to the left. This minor road (Snowhill Lane) climbs to cross
the M6 motorway, and curves up to a junction at the drive to
Wyresdale Park. In attractive woodland surrounds, remain on the
lane as it swings right to commence a short, steep climb to a junction.*

*Cross the stile ahead, from where a path climbs directly up the fell.
This is colourful country: looking back over the plain observe the
Wyreside Lakes, Heysham power station, Lancaster University,
the M6 motorway, Blackpool Tower, a great sweep of Morecambe
Bay, and the distant Lakeland Fells. To the left, meanwhile, is the*

64

*great Ward's Stone skyline. **Passing a small reservoir, advance to the brow. With a small stand of Scots Pine ahead, the path bears right, bound for the waiting Ordnance column on Nicky Nook.** The reedy pool of The Tarn below makes a fine foreground to Ward's Stone. **Over a crossroads of ways the path surmounts a broad ridge, passing a large cairn before reaching the trig. point.** At 705ft this is the summit of the walk. Ahead now is a fine moorland prospect, with the upper reaches of the river Calder burrowing deep into the folds of Hawthornthwaite Fell and the Bleasdale Moors.*

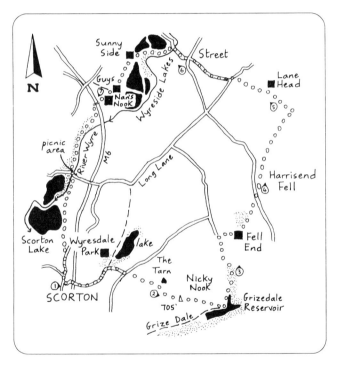

*The path continues away towards a wall. Ignore the ladder-stile and turn down the near side, at once reaching the edge of a steep drop. This is a glorious moment, with Grizedale Reservoir shimmering below in the wooded bowl of Grize Dale. Savour Nicky Nook's finest hour, especially when resplendent in autumn colours. **Descend the clear path to arrive at a stile onto a solid track.** If*

65

wanting to sample Grize Dale in full, and enjoy a shorter walk, turn right here to tramp its length before returning to Scorton village: indeed, with time on your hands it is worth wandering along the valley for a while before returning to this point. Grize Dale - like other such valleys in the north - comes from 'gris' dale, meaning valley of the wild pigs. **Resuming the main route, turn left along the shore, quickly reaching the end of the reservoir's upper arm, and entering woodland.**

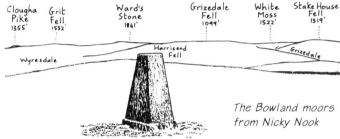

The Bowland moors
from Nicky Nook

Emerging, the track runs on - *over an oddly sited bridge* - **to arrive at a road end. Turn down the drive to Fell End Farm,** *the house almost lost amidst its barns.* **Entering its confines, turn up the right side of the house to the upper yard to gain access to the foot of Harrisend Fell. Here stakes send you half-left up the rough moor to the top corner of a plantation, continuing up onto the moorland road to Oakenclough.** *Of the extensive panorama there is little new, though the retrospect of Nicky Nook is a worthwhile addition.*

Cross straight over, the waymarked path runs along to the left, maintaining its contour as the road drops away. Curving gently around the moor and up to a brow, the views increase over upper Wyresdale. **When the thin path reaches a fence corner, turn down the near side with Foxhouses Brook, to shortly leave the moor at a stile. Continue down by a rough track to reach a farm drive. Turn down this green track between gorse banks to emerge onto a lane.**

Grizedale Reservoir, Nicky Nook

Go left to a junction and then fork right. This soon descends to a crossroads at Street. Advance a little further to Street Bridge on the Wyre. Across, turn down the bank, a path running pleasantly downstream before entering Fox's Wood. On the right here are the Wyreside Lakes, recently transformed into a fishery from old gravel beds by the Duchy of Lancaster. **At a stile the path leaves the woodland for the access road.** The path remaining inside the wood is a permissive route made available by the estate: it returns between Sunnyside and Wyre Lakes to rejoin the path further on. **Turn left along the rough road to reach the car park at Sunny Side.**

Cross to a ladder-stile at the far corner, enjoying views over the lakes to the two fells of the walk. **Cross the field to another stile, then bear left to Guys Farm, ahead. A stile left of the buildings leads out onto a road-end. Turn right past the front of the house -** Lancashire county Girl Guides' centre - **and turn quickly left along the drive to Nan's Nook. Take a gate to the right of the house and cross a couple of fields to a motorway footbridge.** If bearable, pause to enjoy an outstanding panorama of the walk's environs.

On the other side turn sharp left to the start of a large field enclosed by trees. Head across it in the company of a tiny stream, (how quickly the pulsating motorway is forgotten!) **crossing it at the end to reach a stile as the trees close in. A super woodland path crosses to gain the bank of the Wyre, now followed downstream all the way back to Cleveley Bridge:** part of this section is along the embankment of a former mill-race that once supported a cotton factory. **Emerging onto the road, cross the bridge to return to the car park.**

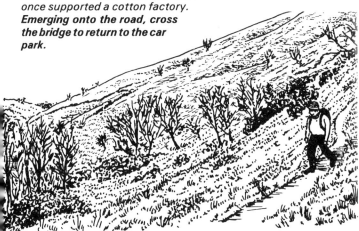

14

WARD'S STONE

START Abbeystead   Grid ref. SD 563543

DISTANCE 13 miles

ORDNANCE SURVEY MAPS
1:50,000
Landranger 102 - Preston & Blackpool
1:25,000
Outdoor Leisure 41 - Forest of Bowland & Ribblesdale

ACCESS   Start from a small parking area by Stoops Bridge at the east end of the hamlet: the road is signed 'Doeholme'. Abbeystead is served by bus from Lancaster.

• ACCESS AREA:The walk makes use of Clougha access area and a linear access strip. These are closed on a number of days during the grouse shooting season (not Sundays) and also at times of high fire risk. If in doubt, contact the Countryside Service (see page110). Restrictions include 'no dogs'.

This classic moorland trek to the summit of Bowland demands a settled day to savour the outstanding views. A word of caution too: more so than any other within these pages, this walk leads into unfrequented and rough terrain, there being no especially easy ways out in an emergency. In poor conditions it is a serious undertaking.

☐   *Abbeystead takes its name from a short-lived involvement with the estates of Furness Abbey. Today it remains a tiny but architecturally interesting private hamlet. A school was founded in 1674: look also for the pinfold. Below the village is the large Abbeystead Lake, constructed in 1853 to supply water for mills down on the Wyre plains. The Duke of Westminster's estate office administers a near 20,000 acres of jealously guarded grouse moor.*

Cross the bridge towards the hamlet, leaving at once by a stile on the right just past a gate. A carriageway shadows the Tarnbrook Wyre upstream. Ahead, a first glimpse of the day's high level antics can be seen in the form of the Ward's Stone skyline. **Through a second pasture the track runs on to a road just above Grizedale Bridge.** To the right is Lower Lee House, dating from 1694 and once an inn. **Turn up the road for almost two miles, early gradients soon easing above the attractive farmhouse of Higher Lea.** Open views become the order of the day. Entirely dominant is the walk to come, with the first moorland objective, Grit Fell, now in the picture directly ahead. The skyline to the right runs along to Ward's Stone.

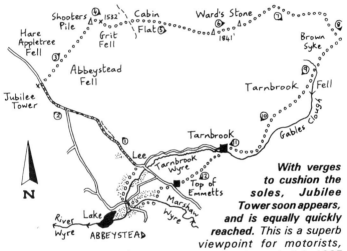

With verges to cushion the soles, Jubilee Tower soon appears, and is equally quickly reached. This is a superb viewpoint for motorists, though is largely superfluous to the panorama. It was built in 1887 by James Harrison of nearby Hare Appletree to commemorate Queen Victoria's Golden Jubilee. Steps give access to a viewing platform, though Grit Fell's slopes are all too evident with or without it. First feature noticed is likely to be Heysham nuclear power station, incongruously sat amongst the many charms of Morecambe Bay. Also prominent are Lancaster University, Grange over Sands, and the whole of south Lakeland, so it seems. Nearer to hand, the plains of the Wyre stretch out to the Fylde Coast.

Turning your back, a chain of paths head through a reedy area and up the fence-side, making steady progress on the rough grass of Hare Appletree Fell. There is much moisture hereabouts, but concentrate on the skyline beacon and it will eventually get nearer.

69

Over the fence the heathery grouse moors of Abbeystead Fell stretch interminably away. An inscribed boundary stone is passed, and **easier contours precede a final pull to the 7ft cairn of Shooters Pile on its rash of stones.** The panorama now extends north, adding Dales mountains over the hinterland of neighbouring Clougha Pike, and an extensive Lakeland skyline beyond the Lune Valley.

Jubilee Tower

Two minutes further along the flat top is a sharp angle of a fence. Here access notices abound, as we trade Clougha access area for the Ward's Stone access strip. A notice informs that it is 7½ miles to Grit Fell, when its top is in fact a minute's walk away! When we eventually reach the other end, its twin will of course be right, so for now, substitute 'Tarnbrook' for 'Grit Fell'. **Cross the stile by another boundary stone and trace the path away through the heather: we are virtually atop Grit Fell from the outset. Ahead, Ward's Stone looks quite a size and quite a distance. The path heads for it through a sea of heather: intermittent cairns and stakes are found throughout this access strip, though at various peaty sections it is not quite infallible.**

All around are rolling moors, though the wilderness aspect is dampened on meeting a solid shooters' track in the saddle of Cabin Flat. Notices warn to keep off it, you'll have to perform an Olympic leap so as not to encroach. **Beyond, small pools are passed before a short pull through the beckoning stone-capped scarp that heralds arrival on the summit plateau. Just ahead is OS column S4996, first of two on this curious top. Just past it is Ward's Stone itself,** a grand outcrop on which to scramble, and also a useful shelter.

The 360° panorama is one to take in slowly: Three Peaks country, Lakeland, Morecambe Bay, and of course the complete mass of Bowland itself. Having surveyed this, thoughts turn to the girth of the plateau. **On setting off for the East top, the path immediately becomes faint: the easiest walking of this moorland route leads directly across to the far side, past one or two peat castles, pools, and an occasional cairn.** This crossing engenders a feeling of being not merely on a moor-top, but also a real fell.

In clear weather the second OS column (2981) is quickly reached, on the corresponding eastern edge. Looking back, doesn't that first column now appear lower? In fact, the Ordnance map claims this point as one metre higher than the first, though Ward's Stone itself might have something to say. Either way, you have traversed the crest of Bowland. The main change in the view is the replacement of the coastal scene with a better picture of Three Peaks country. In the immediate environs are outcrops labelled the Grey Mare and Foal, surmounted by a cairn and a stake.

Head away eastward again, past a cross set in a cairn and then dropping a short way to an acute fence angle. Perched neatly inside is the Queen's Chair, a miniature 'bridestone' with a benchmark carved on top. *Follow the right hand fence away, over a knoll to a junction with a wall.* Enjoy throughout this the scene presented by Ingleborough and its colleagues. *Turn right with the wall on a grassy path, heather on the other side soon crossing to envelop us.* Shortly after, on a brow just before a bend, espy over the wall a prominent pair of great boulders marked as Grey Crag, a more suitable mare and foal.

The way winds on and gradually down in no haste: a fence takes over before encountering peatier sections. This runs on to a corner where a wall takes up the running again. From a grassy corner pause to survey the Hornby Road crossing Salter Fell to the north.

Shooters Pile,
looking to Clougha Pike

In time, fence replaces wall again at a stile, suggesting the north side be followed through much peat, assisted by cairns and stakes pre-dating the boundary fence. Another ladder-stile is reached at Brown Syke, lowest point of the saddle. Ahead is the tempting prospect of the stony fell of Wolfhole Crag, but **our skyline walk is over. Leave the watershed and turn sharp right as indicated by stakes, a decent path heads off for a long return to the valley by way of Tarnbrook Fell.**

East top,
Ward's Stone

Here one might encounter the gulls that nest nearby, adding variety to the call of grouse and other moorland birds. The grouse must have called less happily here on the 'Glorious' Twelfth of 1915, when, with tens of thousands of young men dying in distant trenches, a record bag of almost 3000 birds was claimed. The fell was subjected to further barrages when used for army training during the second almighty conflict. Uncontrollable fires in August 1947 supposedly put paid to any unexploded shells remaining!

Soon a stream comes in to accompany our path. Remain with it, encountering a three-slab footbridge and a chirpy confluence. Cutting a little corner join the main brook - Tarnbrook Wyre - at a splendid location, immediately above a waterfall into a deep pool. After viewing it **cross above it,** and linger awhile where the brook breaks through a tight rocky passage to leave the moors for the dale. **The remains of a hut against a rock wall signal the start of a well made path contouring away, a grand terrace above the brook:** up to the right is a line of jumbled rocks.

The terminus of a shooters' track is reached to encourage big strides down expansive heather slopes. Over to the right the boulders of Long Crag curves endlessly away. Across broadening Gables Clough is the White Side of Tarnbrook Fell, referring to its grassy nature in contrast to the peaty terrain of our own Black Side. Lower down, features of interest by the brook are a fine stand of Scots Pine; and then a sheepfold complex consisting of 16 walled pens. **At the intake wall the track is ushered right to meet a farm drive and access notices. The track runs pleasantly on to meet the road in the hamlet of Tarnbrook.**

One is loathe to disturb the peace of this old Quaker settlement, once much busier when felt hats and gloves were manufactured here. **Unless forging straight on along the road for a quicker finish, locate a green way slipping down to the left opposite a large green. It leads to a concrete bridge over the Tarnbrook Wyre. From a stile behind it the way, initially a green track, runs waymarked across the fields behind Ouzel Thorn Farm. Crossing a field-access lane head away to a barn, crossing to a stile in the far corner to resume this near straight line. Rising to a brow, the way traces a reedy line to a stile at the far end, with Top of Emmetts Farm just ahead. Go left from the stile a few yards to another, then trace the snaking fence to the farm.** In medieval times there was a vaccary (cattle ranch) here. **A stile leads onto its drive and out to the road.**

Cross to a stile and across to a telegraph pole, then down the field-side to a gateway. Just beyond is a crossroads of paths: go left to a prominent ladder-stile, one of two accessing a drive into the wooded grounds of Abbeystead. **Across the drive descend a steep bank, through gorse and trees to a footbridge on the Marshaw Wyre. On the bank above, turn downstream outside the attractive grounds of Abbeystead.** This enormous house was built in 1886 for the Earl of Sefton. Its bold Elizabethan-style front overlooks its extensive grounds and is well seen from our path.

Further downstream another footbridge takes us back over the river. Below here, amid much woodland, the two founders of the Wyre finally merge to form the main river itself, just prior to its entry into Abbeystead Lake. **Turn left down the field, and on reaching a gate in a corner enclosure enter the woods for a few yards to emerge back at the start.**

Moorland falls on the Tarnbrook Wyre

15

CLOUGHA PIKE

START Quernmore   Grid ref. SD 526604

DISTANCE 5 miles

ORDNANCE SURVEY MAPS
1:50,000
Landranger 97 - Kendal to Morecambe
            102 - Preston & Blackpool
1:25,000
Outdoor Leisure 41 - Forest of Bowland & Ribblesdale

ACCESS   Start from the Birk Bank car park on Rigg Lane, 1 mile north-east of Quernmore crossroads. Quernmore is served by bus from Lancaster.

• ACCESS AREA: The opening section of this walk, as far as Clougha Pike, is within Clougha access area. This is closed on a number of days (not Sundays) from August12th (the first month of the grouse shooting season is the busiest time) and at times of high fire risk. Restrictions include 'no dogs'. If in doubt, contact the Countryside Service, see page 110.

☐ *Take the stile by an access notice at the back of the car park and follow the track away. The rocky bank ahead is regenerating from the activities of the Birk Bank Quarry. 250 years ago, Clougha slate was in great demand for roofing. At a fork bear right, then right again on a track running to a gate. Don't go through, but take a path down to the left, where duckboards cross a marsh to a stile.*

A well used path starts to climb the fell, initially through oakwood and alongside a beck: grand stuff. Rising past the great bank of the old quarry, the path firms up to climb to a wall junction beneath a rocky knoll. Here is a choice of stiles. That to the right sends a more direct route to the top, while that to the left is now described.

Over it we enter the atmospheric confines of Windy Clough. Whilst one can meander along the bottom throughout its length, finest option is to take a branch path left within a few yards of the stile. This winds up to the wall on the rocky crest. A thin trod runs along this smashing little ridge atop a notable gritstone edge, looking dramatically over the clough to the rising slopes of Clougha. *A patch of oakwood at the end leads to a wall-corner. In the absence of a stile turn down the ankle-twisting slope with the wall to a ladder-stile at the head of the clough. Across it simply follow the wall up to the right: initially extremely steep and intermittently rocky, it is virtually a mini-scramble.*

Things ease up in the heather above, as the thin trod clings to the wall. A smaller amphitheatre precedes two pronounced notches, both offering further simple scrambling if taken directly. At the

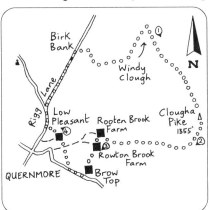

second of these the path cuts a wall-corner to a ladder-stile, where a path joins in from the right. Returning to the wall, yet another path joins us, and the way now rises only ever steadily. Throughout this easy ascent the views are magnificent, over Quernmore's vale to the silvery waters of Morecambe Bay. Behind are the shapely heights of Lakeland, presenting a full skyline to survey.

The wall falters at the onset of a rocky edge. Over to the left a fence branches off, taking a path with it. The finest route remains on the edge, the walking being along a flat, stony pavement. A large cairn heralds the final stage to the waiting summit. An Ordnance column (S4999) shares the platform with a large, sprawling cairn, while a brace of useful shelters take advantage of the rash of stones. As a viewpoint it offers little in addition to the scene that has been enjoyed for the last hour, save for the inclusion of more moorland. The fact that level ground heads away to the heathery hinterland is no real disappointment on our 'pikeless' pike!

The clearest path heading away is one running east to the fence, bound for Grit Fell. **Our way off heads south a few yards before becoming distinct as it slants down the fellside. Leaving the stones and heather behind it continues to slant down the fell, sometimes rather faintly. Apart from the odd marshy section it remains entirely pleasant, crossing Rowton Brook and swinging down to a gateway at an access notice. It runs directly downhill now, parallel to the brook,** *and for the most part both are in superb form - the tinkling brook offers a temptation to linger and dangle feet on a hot summer's day.* **The last stage descends a large enclosure to Rooten Brook Farm. Head down the yard and out by the drive:** *if omitting the chance of refreshment at Brow Top, simply follow the drive all the way down to the road at Quernmore.*

Clougha Pike from the north

Otherwise, **turn left immediately after leaving the yard, crossing the field-top beneath the house,** *which bears a 1693 datestone.* **A tiny footbridge crosses the brook, from where two stiles lead to the drive of neighbouring Rowton Brook:** *confused? - so is the postman.* **Turn up into the yard, leaving by a small gate at the top side of the house.** *From the stile behind pause to look at the house-side sporting a fully slated defence.* **Ahead now is Brow Top. Cross the field to a stile where fence and wall meet, and head along to enter its confines by another stile beyond a set of pens.** *Here a view* indicator points out such features as Blackpool Tower and Heysham power station, and more endearing landmarks such as Black Combe across Morecambe Bay. It also relates the legend of Quernmore. The name, incidentally, comes from querns, or millstones, hewn from the local rock for the grinding of corn. Some versions are on display in the grounds. In other instances the name has evolved into Whern, as in Whernside in the Yorkshire Dales.

Usually open from Easter to October, Brow Top offers various attractions, though the most appealing at this moment is likely to be the cafe. There is also a crafts centre, while the younger end might be drawn by the prospect of the farm visitor centre and the activity toys. In season, new born lambs can be inspected.

Its drive runs out to a road. Turn downhill, enjoying views over this 'upland' valley of the river Conder. *Half-way down to the sharp bend take a stile on the right, and slant down through a large gap in the wall, continuing down to join a road (the Rooten farms' drive). Take the gate in front and down a walled track to Low Pleasant Farm.* Quernmore is seen just across to the left. *As the drive swings sharp left go straight ahead, through a tiny enclosure alongside a cottage. Slant down the field to a gate onto Rigg Lane.* It was around here that Roman kilns - or hypocausts - have been discovered, complete with bricks, tiles and pots still in the ovens.

Turn right along the road, soon forking right again to follow the narrow lane back to the start, enjoying views of the Clougha slopes and with Quernmore church tower seen down to the left.

Clougha Pike

16

LITTLEDALE

START Little Cragg   Grid ref. SD 546617

DISTANCE 6½ miles

ORDNANCE SURVEY MAPS
1:50,000
Landranger 97 - Kendal to Morecambe
1:25,000
Outdoor Leisure 41 - Forest of Bowland & Ribblesdale

ACCESS Little Cragg car park is on a minor road linking Brookhouse and Quernmore via Littledale. Approach from Brookhouse (off the A683 at Caton; bus service from Lancaster) by Littledale Road (2½ miles from the village).

• ACCESS AREA: The final stage of the walk enters the Clougha access area, which is closed for a number of days (not Sundays) from August 12th (the first month of the grouse shooting season is the busiest time) and at times of high fire risk. If it should be closed, a simple (shorter) alternative finish is available. One of the access area's restrictions is 'no dogs'.

◻ *Having already enjoyed grand views while pulling your boots on, head east from the car park back towards Brookhouse. Through a cattle-grid with Cragg Farm on the right, note the attractive east front of the farmhouse. The narrow road winds down through rough pasture, enjoying fine views up Littledale.*

This minor road becomes enclosed again to descend to the charming wooded surrounds of the meeting of Udale and Artle Becks. Udale Bridge and Fostal Bridge are crossed in succession, passing Littledale scout camp down to the left before a short pull leads up and along to a crossroads at New House Farm.

Turn right here, passing the farmhouse of Crossgill (Crossghyll on its nameplate) with a 1681 datestone: another pleasing house stands before the drive to Littledale Hall. Just past it is the tiny church of St Ann, Littledale's former place of worship. Dating from 1751, it is now a private dwelling. **Beyond is a hairpin bend: advance through a stile onto a green pathway between plantations. At the end keep straight on, the obvious way approaching a church sat in the middle of a field.**

This 'Free Church' of 1849 was attached to nearby Littledale Hall. Now merely a shell, its intact stonework and timber ceiling are appreciated by the sheep that find sanctuary within. After the evidence of the last ten minutes one is apt to think The Almighty has fallen from favour in Littledale! At the back is a solitary grave. The intact one of two slabs marks the resting place of father and son Dodsons of the hall, the unfortunate son having beaten his father here by 31 years. **Just beyond, the track forks: the main one drops down to Littledale Hall, to which we shall shortly return.**

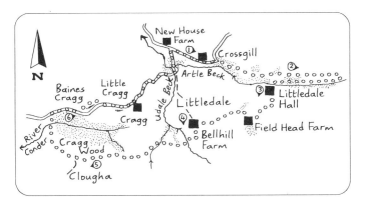

For now however, take the branch up to the left. Remain along the field-top when the track goes through a gate, and keep on to a little gate to run inside the top of a wooded bank. *The local parish has a rights of way group actively improving the paths hereabouts.* **Emerging, a grand scene greets the eye with the beck splashing along beneath woodland: our return route is seen below, but for now resist it and keep straight on, crossing a tiny stream and generally traversing along the bracken bank. At the end the path winds down to a beck. In this lovely location we turn about. Strictly speaking, the path fords the beck to a gate and then turns on the**

*brow behind to drop back down to a stile in the wall. A collapsed footbridge by the stile was being put to the torch immediately after my crossing, and will probably be replaced at some stage - not that one is really needed. **Now simply head downstream, returning through the patch of woodland to reach the bridge at Littledale Hall.***

The old church,
Littledale Hall

Cross to the attractive coach house and turn away from the hall, up to the farmyard. *The hall is currently used by a religious group.* **At the last barn at the top of the yard, leave the track by a gate on the right. A muddy track runs briefly upstream through park-like grounds with Foxdale Beck. Quickly crossing it by a footbridge, a path doubles back to wind up the bank. Leaving the trees at a stile, turn right along the fence-side. A wall takes over to head towards Field Head Farm. Well before it take a stile in the wall and head round the right side of the buildings to gain the drive. Following this away it runs over a brow and down to Bellhill Farm.**

Cross the cattle-grid and turn into the yard, below the short drive to the house. At the far end go through a small enclosure and head down the left side of the field on a rough track. Turn sharp right at the bottom to a ford on the side beck, but don't cross it. Instead, ford it a few yards downstream to reach a footbridge over the more substantial Udale Beck. Rise away with the wall to a gate in the fence that takes over, from where a green track rises above the belt of trees and along the field-top. At the end a stone bridge crosses Sweet Beck, and just up behind it an inviting branch left sends a link path to the Clougha access area. *If this be closed, remain on the track to Skelbow barn, and along field-sides (over the Conder-Littledale col) to be back at the start within ten minutes.* **Otherwise, turn up the track which rises pleasantly to a stile and runs along to a ladder-stile and access notice at the foot of the moor.**

Turn right, crossing the burbling stream - named from birth as the river Conder - *to the prominent green way slanting away.* Over to the right both Baines Cragg and, hopefully, the car should be seen. Intervening are Cragg Wood and the infant Conder valley. *A slimmer green branch right near the top leads onto a heathery edge above the marshy beck, from where a second stream is crossed, and the edge followed to a point where a clear broad track rises to the edge. This then runs across the moor, becoming a thinner trod running along to a point above a prominent group of rocks. This proves to be the colourful head of a little gill* - a grand spot on a sunny, late summer day, *and the trod runs on past it to join a newly laid shooters' track.* Ahead is Lancaster's Ashton Memorial, behind which are Morecambe Bay and the more distant Lakeland Fells.

Turn down the track as it winds through a gateway and down to a gate and stile with access notices. Approaching a house, don't take its drive out but go right over a slab bridge to a stile, where a thin path climbs a gorse bank to a ladder-stile onto a lane. Turn right up here alongside lovely Cragg Wood to reach Baines Cragg. This small patch of open country is no longer an 'official' access area, though people still see it as an alternative to the road. Just yards into it, a thin path rises left, crossing to the start of the knoll and leading a delightful course along the crest, a real natural playground for kids - of all ages. In autumn this has to be seen to be believed, as a colourful foreground leads the eye to Cragg Wood beneath rough moorland slopes: in the other direction are the Lune

Valley and the Lakeland Fells. **This brilliant conclusion to the walk winds back down to the road at the end, with the car park just beyond, over the cattle-grid.**

Baines Cragg, looking to Little Cragg

17

ROEBURNDALE

START Wray   Grid ref. SD 604679

DISTANCE 9 miles

ORDNANCE SURVEY MAPS
1:50,000
Landranger 97 - Kendal to Morecambe
          98 - Wensleydale & Upper Wharfedale (just)
1:25,000
Outdoor Leisure 41 - Forest of Bowland & Ribblesdale

ACCESS Start from a riverside parking area at the east entrance
to the village, just off the B6480, by the modern bridge. One
could also start from the main street itself. Wray is served by
Lancaster-Bentham buses.

*Wray and the Roeburn are indelibly linked, the river supplying water
power for an industrious past. Attractive cottages line its streets,
including a larger than average number of yeoman houses: a
particularly old one (of many that are seen) is inscribed 'RP 1656',
referring to Richard Pooley who founded the school. There is also
a Friends' Meeting House of 1704.*

☐ **Head along to the main street and up past the** George & Dragon
**and the church (Holy Trinity - 1840) noting the ornate street lamp
commemorating Queen Victoria's Golden Jubilee in 1887. At the
Post office turn right up the road to Roeburndale West, and begin
a steep climb of Dick Brow.** *Take a well-earned break to look back
over the village: high beyond is Three Peaks country.* **Easing out for
a while (during which time look over to the right to see Hornby
Castle rising out of the trees) before a second steep pull precedes
a junction with Moor Lane.** *Over to the right is a major length of the
Lune Valley.* **Turn left, inevitably uphill, though the hard work is
almost done.**

On approaching a cattle-grid at Whit Moor Gate seek out an illegible milestone set into the wall on the left. **At the cattle-grid the moor is gained amid vast views over Roeburndale to the high moors.** *Though this road start is not ideal, it has few alternatives, and in any case gets us off to a flier which will be appreciated later in this sizeable walk.*

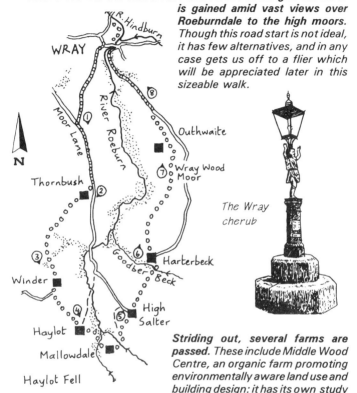

The Wray cherub

Striding out, several farms are passed. *These include Middle Wood Centre, an organic farm promoting environmentally aware land use and building design: it has its own study centre, and runs courses.* **Only leave the road as it starts to drop, at the first farm on the right. Turn up the drive to Thornbush, along the front of the house and up to a gate at the end. Entering a field, the path officially goes straight up to the top corner, but the more obvious way is the track running to the foot of a line of Scots Pine, then up the far side of them.**

From here the track rises more gently left, paralleling a sunken way. *Over to the left is a vast Roeburndale panorama.* **When the track swings sharp right to a gate, go straight on with the channelled way to a solid wall ahead. Go left with it to locate a built-in stile, behind which cross the steep walls enclosing Warm Beck. Once across,**

83

slant left up the rough pasture of Barkin, to reach a gate where two fences meet in a corner. Head away from it with a drain, crossing a collapsed wall as a clear track forms. This runs on beneath a small plantation to the muddy enclosure of Hill Barn, just past which is Winder Farm. This is a very exposed settlement - note the 1673 datestone above the door. *Its drive runs quickly on to a road-end.*

Without setting foot on tarmac, turn through a gate and down a rough road with Haylot Farm visible ahead. Above it rises a taunting moorland skyline, prize feature being the cone of Mallowdale Pike. *Winding steeply down to cross Bladder Stone Beck, the track then rises to the farm. Take a gate to the left of the yard, to enter the field in front of the house. Cross to a gate in the bottom right corner, and descend a small enclosure to a stile at the wall-foot.* Below, a steep wooded bank falls to the winding Roeburn, while across to the right is Mallowdale Farm, with a deep valley intervening: the high moors draw close now.

The Three Peaks from Whit Moor Gate

Head along the bank high above the river, using a stile midway to step inside to enjoy a champagne moment. From here a divine little path winds down the wooded slope, deep into the secret confines. At the bottom a footbridge crosses Mallow Gill, and immediately upstream a delectable watersmeet greets the eye. Forged beneath a green pyramid, this is a place to linger, and worth every yard of that early road walking. .

Penance is swift: behind, bear initially right on a part-evident path winding up the steep bank to Mallowdale Farm. Enter by a gate to the left and pass along the front, turning into the yard to emerge on its drive. With grand views high into the upper reaches of the Roeburn, *this winds down to Mallowdale Bridge, the walk's turning point. Double back up the opposite slope to a barn.* Pause here to appraise Mallowdale's peerless setting under the edge of the moor. *Up to the right, meanwhile, is High Salter, and from the gate opposite, head up the field to the farming hamlet. Keep right of all buildings to a gateway onto the Hornby Road or Salters Way (see WALK 22), here enjoying its final unsurfaced yards.*

Turn down it, but leave almost at once by a gate on the right. Advance through a gateway, and when the wall turns down go with it to a ladder-stile. Ahead, Ingleborough reigns supreme. *Turn right to another, then aim for the far corner, but before reaching it bear left to a step-stile in the fence. Resume to the wall and turn down it to a reedy corner* where a rusting Zephyr makes a semi-permanent landmark. *A corner stile gives access to a large, reedy pasture. Aim right of the buildings of Harterbeck, reaching the top of High Buckbank Wood at a prominent knoll.* This is another superb moment: directly below is a substantial waterfall on Goodber Beck,

deep in trees and lined by scars. Just upstream is a footbridge, and from the knoll one can also see the gentler upper falls. **From the footbridge a green path slants left to run along to the farm, a track becoming enclosed at a slab footbridge and ford to emerge onto the roadhead at the farm entrance.**

Upper falls, Goodber Beck

With the true path impassable, the farmer recommends going right a few yards to the first gate on the left, there advancing along the wall until a gate is crossed to follow a fence-side away. Through a gate at the end a track is joined: this runs down the field-side to demise at a barn. Continue along the front to a conspicuous gap-stile in the wall ahead, to enter a big, reedy pasture. Maintain this line through several walls in various states, until a long, solid wall starts on the right. This remains foolproof company for some time, a long walk giving ample opportunity to enjoy well-wooded Roeburndale views. Over on the right the terrain gives way to the stony Wray Wood Moor, and *at the far end a gateway leads into a more welcoming, slightly stony pasture.*

The map indicates old coal mines on these flanks, and on the brow there is a little evidence of man's work. To the right are open views across to the prow of Burn Moor beyond the intervening Hindburn

85

*valley. **At the next corner a walled way is entered, a short-lived green gem. At the end keep on to the drive to the farming hamlet of Outhwaite just to the left. Turn right over the cattle-grid but leave at once by a stile cleverly built into the wall-corner. Head away with a short length of wall, crossing a streamlet then accompanying its narrow but deep-cut course down to a stile. Continue down to find a conspicuous stile in a tiny wall at the end. Entering a colourful little enclosure, bear right to a gate onto a lane.***

All that remains is to turn downhill, a good mile or so back into Wray. *The way steepens and winds down through woodland, and the attractive environs of Hunt's Gill Beck. Just beyond is a renovated former bobbin mill and a row of workers' cottages. Past here, Kitty Bridge crosses the river for a quick return to the village.* **Remain on the road by the river to reach Wray Bridge,** *alternatively a short-cut field path cuts a tiny corner.*

Built about 1780, Wray Bridge stood firm against floods that wreaked havoc after a freak cloudburst on the moors in August 1967. Its sturdiness only increased the damage as water banked up, and the little green caught the full fury of the devastation. A garden by surviving Bridge End is on the site of five houses that fell victim out of a row of six. **Either return to the main street,** *noting on the right a plethora of old datestones,* **or turn down the green riverbank to see the Roeburn's confluence with the larger Hindburn,** *fitting in view of the theme of our last few hours.* **Continue downstream to return to the riverside area at the bridge,** *which replaced the humped Meal Bank Bridge swept away by the floods.*

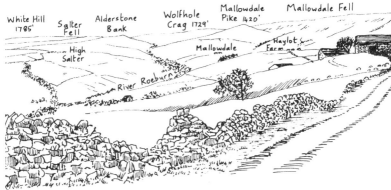

Upper Roeburndale, from above Winder

18

HINDBURN COUNTRY

START Lowgill   Grid ref. SD 653647

DISTANCE 6½ miles

ORDNANCE SURVEY MAPS
1:50,000
Landranger 97 - Kendal to Morecambe
          98 - Wensleydale & Upper Wharfedale
1:25,000
Outdoor Leisure 41 - Forest of Bowland & Ribblesdale

ACCESS Start from the centre of the hamlet. There is limited parking on the wider sections of road above the houses, or alternatively there is a lay-by opposite the church (at the end of the walk, GR 653653). There is further parking just downstream from Mill Bridge.

Lowgill is a small community that has lost shop, Post office, and the Rose & Crown *inn that survived into the 1970s. A Methodist chapel of 1866 sits on a lawn that enjoys a brief spell as a sea of snowdrops, while Lowgill House sports an 18th century datestone.*

☐ *Head up the main street past a tiny green bearing a seat and a war memorial, and up the narrowing road heading up-dale.* With much holly in evidence in the hedgerows, already we enjoy smashing views over the richly wooded Hindburn Valley. Ahead are the high moors enclosing the dale, especially haunting when streaked with snow. ***Crossing Bull Gill, keep straight on at a junction at Ivah to run along to a sharp bend.*** The sections immediately before and just along from here are on the line of the Roman road from Ribchester to Over Burrow in the Lune Valley.

Here, as the road turns downhill, head straight on along a farm road to Swans. Go to a gate left of the house to pass between house and barn, then straight up the tiny bank behind and on to a gate. Beyond

it a faint green track runs along a gnarled hedge, accompanying a sunken way to reach a grassy little bridge and a gate. **Continue along the next field, through a gateway and along to a brow:** below is a fine prospect of the confluence of Middle Gill and Whitray Beck in lovely wooded surrounds. **Continuing, descend left to locate a gate at the foot of a section of wall. Down from it a footbridge on Whitray Beck is reached. Tackling the steep bank behind, a faint, hollowed way leads more amicably up to a wall-corner and a track soon forms to lead directly up to Whitray Farm** (1859 datestone).

Continue through the yard and out on the drive, turning right along this moorfoot road. On the left now are the slopes of Whitray Fell fronting the many untracked miles of Bowland, while ahead is a glimpse of Mallowdale Pike overtopping the intermediate moorland ridge. **We cross Middle Gill, a typical moorland stream burbling down. Just beyond, the road ends abruptly at Botton Head Farm.**

Enter the yard and go immediately right to a gate before reaching the farmhouse. A track aims directly away down the field centre, on a modest tongue that divides the two upper arms of Hindburndale. From a gate at the bottom a sunken way and hedgerow offer company as the track reaches a gate in the bottom corner. This last short stretch is again on the line of the Roman road.

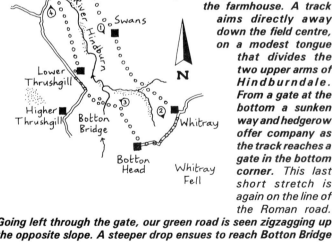

Going left through the gate, our green road is seen zigzagging up the opposite slope. A steeper drop ensues to reach Botton Bridge in a pleasing setting.

Up the other side the track winds, grassed over but with clear evidence of a more solid, previously better used surface. From a gate at the top look back over dale-head country to Whitray and Botton Head, then **advance to join a road through the fields.** Up to the left is Higher Thrushgill, with the only plantation in these parts alongside. **Two minutes along to the right, meanwhile, turn down a drive to Lower Thrushgill. Go left to pass left of the house, along its lawn-side and a very short-lived green way to emerge into a field. Head across to a gate, and on again to a crude stile.** Looking across to the environs of Lowgill, it may be possible to see the line of the Roman road, which is part overlaid by the modern road, a good clue.

From here a fence provides company as we head along another minor tongue. On reaching a wall the first 'real' stile of the day leads into a vast reedy pasture. Continue down, keeping a wooded bank on the right until it subsides: now turn down to the right to approach a sharp crook of the river, with a gate onto a lane just to the left.

On the right the Hindburn flows under Stairend Bridge, and we trace it downstream to a sharp bend just after crossing **Mill Beck.** The former Botton Mill is back up to the left, but **we go through the gate in front.**

A reedy riverside pasture is entered, and a track runs on to cross a stream at the far end. Up to the left is an attractive wooded bank. **Keep on through a longer, unkempt pasture to a gate at the end. Here leave the river by rising to another gate where the track is more defined, passing through a long-collapsed wall. This rises through colourful country to reach a ruinous barn.** Note the prospect of Lowgill directly across the deep-cut, wooded valley.

Middle Gill, Botton Head

89

Up to the left is the great bowl of Helks Wood. **From a gate beyond the barn, traces of a wall lead across to a distinct notch in the bracken slope, with a gate in a line of trees behind. Up the bank behind, don't take the sunken way up to the left, but keep straight on to cross a deeply embowered beck before slanting left up to a gate in front of a crumbling barn. Pass along the front to a gate at the end, then on to a gateway (shared with the stream of Crow Gill) just above a restored barn.**

Cross again to the edge of a deeper set wooded beck, then turn down its near side. At the bottom corner a wall-stile admits to Over Houses Great Wood, and a grand little path winds down to approach the river. Turn downstream a short way from the stile to a footbridge across it. *Like its neighbour the Roeburn (see WALK 17), the Hindburn takes its name, inevitably, from the deer that once commonly frequented these parts.*

Mill Bridge, Lowgill

Turn downstream a few more yards to a kissing-gate, and a flight of steps up a wooded bank. In the field above a track forms to climb to a barn, rising again through a higher field: *over to the right the Helks Wood neighbourhood is prominent.* **Instead of going through the gate at the top, opt for a gate to its left, and head along the top of the initially wooded bank to a gate at the far side:** *the Roman road is crossed yet again here.* **The gate admits to Lowgill Lane: turn right for a direct return to the hamlet, otherwise go left down to Mill Bridge, a lovely spot. Just across it an urban footpath sign points up a narrow lane between buildings, taking a cobbled hairpin just above which is the drive to Lowgill church.**

The church of the Good Shepherd is a stout edifice, its great tower appearing to rest uncomfortably on groaning walls. This present church dates only from 1888, replacing at least two previous chapels. Its stained glass reflects its location and name, which couldn't be more suitable in this isolated farming country. **A stile enters the field parallel to the church drive, continuing on through a gateway at the end to a small enclosure adjacent to the churchyard. For those visiting the church, a gate out of the corner of the yard leads to this enclosure. This leads to the churchgoers' path from the hamlet.** Just behind the church is the former village school: not merely closed like so many rural schools, but happily only replaced, as we shall quickly see.

Before drawing level with the old school, turn down the steep bank where a partly-stepped path winds down to a footbridge in a lovely wooded dell of the Hindburn. Up the other side stay with the right-hand fence, a wall taking over at the top to run along to a corner. As a fence takes over turn through the gate and along a part-enclosed way to approach the hamlet: the modern school is just down to the right. Through a small housing development, advance to a stile to the edge of a farmyard then turn right onto the road.

The Good Shepherd,
Lowgill

91

FOURSTONES

START Bentham   Grid ref. SD 667692

DISTANCE 6½ miles

ORDNANCE SURVEY MAPS
1:50,000
Landranger 98 - Wensleydale & Upper Wharfedale
1:25,000
Outdoor Leisure 41 - Forest of Bowland & Ribblesdale
Outdoor Leisure 2 - Yorkshire Dales West (tiny section only)

ACCESS Start from the centre of town, where the Slaidburn road leaves the Main Street for the railway station. There is a car park behind the main street (above it), signposted up Goodenber Road: pedestrian alleyways lead directly back onto the main street. Bentham is served by the Skipton-Lancaster railway line, and by Lancaster-Settle/Ingleton buses.

This walk ambles round the ancient Forest of Mewith, and boasts the objective of the walk as its summit.

❑ *From Main Street descend the road past the railway station to the bridge over the Wenning. Across, a driveway heads downstream to a house at Moulterbeck. Pass between the buildings to a gate, then turn up left to locate a stile into the wood. A lovely path climbs narrow confines, passing a waterslide before emerging. Continue up the field to a stile, there going left on a broad track to the rear of the buildings at Brookhouse. Advance through two gates, and from the second turn sharp right up the field to a stile at the top.* Already Ingleborough makes a magnificent prospect behind, and will remain so for most of the walk. **Continue up and along to a fence corner, running on to approach Bowker House. A muddy lane (circumvented by a stile to the left) leads between the farm buildings and out along its drive.**

Cross straight over the back lane to a gate, and climb the field to the house at Flannagill. From a stile onto its drive, turn along the house front and up to a stile in the garden wall. The expansive grassy moorland of Bents is entered, and climbed pleasurably with the aid of sheeptrods. On the skyline ahead, the Great Stone of Fourstones cannot be missed. This is our goal, and a couple of farm drives are crossed en route, the reedy terrain being largely dry.

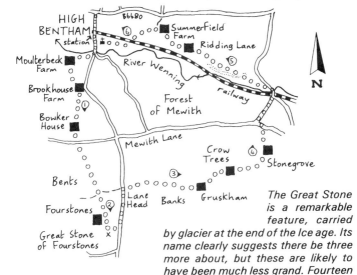

The Great Stone is a remarkable feature, carried by glacier at the end of the Ice age. Its name clearly suggests there be three more about, but these are likely to have been much less grand. Fourteen steps hewn out of it make an 'ascent' obligatory, while one might effect a traverse using less crafted steps on the north-east side. From above or below, however, the view is superb, an extensive panorama embracing a massive sweep of Three Peaks country across the Wenning farmland. Nearer to hand the rolling Bowland moors cut off more distant prospects. **A path - zealously reinforced with boardwalks - doubles back to the Slaidburn road, which is followed north.** *Ingleborough's proud stance remains a magnet.*

At Lane Head the road becomes enclosed at a cattle-grid, but before that turn right along a rough drive. This ends at the second house, so cross the ravine of Burbles Gill by a simple bridge and head directly across the moorland of Banks. *This seems quite an expanse until you consider the vast sprawl of Burn Moor rising above, itself just one small corner of the great moorland massif of*

Bowland. *Continuing east a broad track is met at a wall, with a water authority installation just below. The drive runs on to Gruskham, second house along. Take a gate immediately in front of the house (redundant hand-gate alongside) to descend to one at the field-bottom, then go right with the wall to reach Gill Beck.*

A slab-bridge crosses the tree-lined beck and the way advances on to a stile in the next wall. A wall heads away to Crow Trees: cross its drive to a gate, then across a beck in a shady enclosure to a stile in an old fence. Continue away over a tiny brow to a solid stile, and head away with the wall. Take a gate in it and rise to a gentle knoll, then veer away from the wall to locate a stile in the fence opposite.

Without using the stile, turn down the field-side on a track that forms to descend to Stonegrove, following the farm drive down to Mewith Lane. Go left a few yards and turn down Brow Lane to a junction at the railway bridge. Cross both this and the bridge over the Wenning and take a stile on the left. Turn downstream past a solitary oak to a stile behind, then cross to another wall stile before slanting right to a gap in the wooded bank. Running along the top side of the wood, several fields are crossed before, at the wood end, slanting right up to a wall-stile amidst a thick hedge. Cross to a track with the farm of Ridding Lane directly ahead, passing the barn of Low Linghaw (1691 datestone on the side) to the farm.

Enter the yard but instead of ascending its drive, advance to a gate into a field. Cross to a stile and slant up the next field, continuing up another then to a top corner stile in front of a house. Go left along the enclosure in front, and with Bentham appearing directly ahead cross another small field to a near-hidden gap-stile. A green lane is entered, which immediately becomes pedestrian only for its short duration. At the end ignore the stile ahead, and take one on the left to descend the field-side past a wooded bank to the railway. Cross with care and turn right along the field top, parallel with the line to pass left of the church (St. Margarets, 1837) to emerge back onto the road between the station and the bridge.

The Great Stone of Fourstones

20

WENNINGDALE

START Bentham   Grid ref. SD 667689

FINISH Clapham (railway station)

DISTANCE 7 miles

ORDNANCE SURVEY MAPS
1:50,000
Landranger 98 - Wensleydale & Upper Wharfedale
1:25,000
Outdoor Leisure 41 - Forest of Bowland & Ribblesdale

ACCESS Start from the railway station on the Lancaster-Skipton line: the better parking facilities at Clapham suggest starting there, if coming by car, and catching the train before the walk. Bentham and Clapham are also linked by the Lancaster-Settle bus. Bentham has a car park above the main street, off Goodenber Road.

□ *From the railway station take the road down to the bridge over the Wenning. Across, turn immediately left along a narrow lane. As it parts company with the Wenning, take a stile on the left before the houses and head through the fields, a generally faint but obvious way running parallel with the river. After several fields, as the river returns for brief company, head through a crumbling gateway and aim for the farm of Staggarth ahead. A gate into its yard sees us through to the far end, where an iron stile gives access to the field behind.*

Rising away, a faint path slants up to a stile by a gate at the top corner. Above it a wooded bank is gained. Earlier, a steep wooded drop falls to the river, providing a glorious prospect of its meanderings far below: Ingleborough is majestic behind. *As the trees turn off continue up the field, and at the top go left below the wall. A well placed seat tempts one to pause and survey the fine prospect of Ingleborough, one that will remain for the greater part of the walk.*

At the end advance to the ruin of Dawson Close, beyond which a slab bridge leads to a neat squeezer-stile. From it slant up the field to a stile in the far corner, then bear left to another corner-stile. Behind it a path runs above the burbling Gill Beck and on to a little footbridge. Across, rise to a wall-stile just above, then bear up the left side of the large field to a stile onto Mewith Lane, adjacent to New House.

Go left past a road junction and turn up the farm drive to Stonegrove. Passing through the yard and up by the house, the track rises into a field. As the surface falls away, continue up the fence-side to locate a stile in it. Cross it and head directly away to a stile in the wall behind, which precedes the steep wooded bank of Badger Ford Beck. A small foot-bridge leads to a similar bank on the other side. This attractive setting derives its name from the 'badger', a travelling corn dealer.

At the brow, cross to a stile in the corner to enter a vast pasture. Aim for the build-ings in the trees ahead, and a farm drive is joined to run along to Mewith Head Hall. A mere field's-length above are Burn Moor's bracken clad flanks.

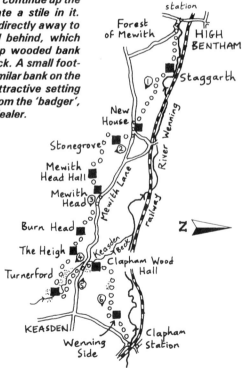

Enter the confines of the hall and cross the spacious yard to pass along the front of the house. *Dating from the early 18th century when it was clearly of greater importance, its impressive facade is well seen - note the sundial high above the door.*

Mewith Head Hall

At the far side by a barn, take the right-hand gate and cross the field to a stile. Continue on to a gate left of a barn to enter a green lane climbing the last few yards onto the open fell. *This colourful open country is not for us, inviting as it is.* **Instead, turn down to Mewith Head Farm, through a jumble of buildings and out along its drive onto Mewith Lane.**

Turn right, the road at once becoming unenclosed. Ignoring the first footpath sign along a broad track, advance a further 150 yards to the next such sign. Scale the bracken knoll of Cinder Hill and continue away. A trod ends when the bracken does, but keep straight on, south-east, through wet, tussocky terrain. In mist this seems an endless wasteland, though within five minutes you'll reach Bloe Beck. A tiny slab is superfluous to its crossing, beyond which stiles in quick succession precede a rise to Burn Head Farm.

Two gates in front of a bungalow lead to the farm drive. Go along the front of the farmhouse to a small gate behind an out-house, then cross the field to a hand-gate at the far end. Continue to a footbridge over Ratton Syke in an obvious gap in the trees, and rise similarly obviously towards the next farm, The Heigh. Without entering its yard, go beneath all the buildings to a gate immediately below the lowest of them. Cross straight over the drive and rise away on a gravel track as far as a gate. Here halt the climb by squeezing through a stile by a gate on the left, and head away with the wall. Beyond a fence the wall turns away: here slant up to a characterful boulder-field above the equally attractive Stony Wood.

At the end of stones and trees descend to High Head Gill, finding a gap-stile in a tiny section of wall. Rising away to the left, an old wall and ditch lead around to a stile by a gate. The ditch and mound continue away, dropping slightly as a track forms to become enclosed and descend to Turnerford Farm. Pass round the front of the buildings and out to the bridge over Keasden Beck. The quickest conclusion follows the drive up onto the road, turning right to a moorland crossroads near the one-time Keasden Methodist chapel and then descending over Clapham Moor to the river Wenning and the railway station.

Single-slab footbridge

98

More enjoyably, turn immediately downstream from a stile after the bridge, to trace the winding course of the Wenning down to Reebys Lane. After a wooded bank on a bend the first fence offers a small obstacle: beyond, all is plain sailing. A natural impasse, however, adds interest in the form of a steep, unnegotiable bank that must be risen above before two attractive beckside pastures lead down to a gate onto a road. Go left, still in the company of the beck to a pleasant corner at an arched bridge.

Without crossing turn down the drive to white-walled Clapham Wood Farm, taking a gate to the right of the buildings. A green track climbs above the rear of the house to a set of gates and waymarks. Open views return, with, inevitably, Ingleborough reappearing. **Opt for the left hand gate and follow a wall towards a barn. Keeping left of it, descend a wall-side to a stile onto a drive. Go right along here past a small wood,** with a view now of hotel, station, and, quickly appearing, Clapham Viaduct. High above it, the table-topped limestone height of Moughton is prominent on the Dales skyline.

The track turns sharply down to Wenning Side Farm. Entering its yard, take the first right turn out of it into a field, and cross to the far corner. Again, the right-hand of adjacent gates is used, and again a wall followed away. On the brow pause to note Ingleborough's change of angle - its cutaway profile lost as its rounded shoulder of Little Ingleborough steps in. The twin-like sentinels of Pot Scar and Smearsett Scar break the skyline much further to the right.

From a stile at the end advance to a gate at Giffords Farm, and going right a few yards a stile leaves the drive for a short-cut down to the road junction at Wenning Bank Bridge: an old West Riding sign remains in place. **Cross the bridge and up under the rail line to reach the station and hotel, in whichever order you prefer.**

The old Methodist chapel, Keasden

21

WHELP STONE CRAG

START Giggleswick   Grid ref. SD 803628

DISTANCE 9½ miles

ORDNANCE SURVEY MAPS
1:50,000
Landranger 98 - Wensleydale & Upper Wharfedale
          103 - Blackburn & Burnley
1:25,000
Outdoor Leisure 41 - Forest of Bowland & Ribblesdale

ACCESS Start from Giggleswick station on the Morecambe-Leeds line. There is a British Rail car park, and a lay-by just back on the road. The village centre and Settle are a good mile up the road past the Station Hotel. Both are also served by bus from Skipton and Ingleton/Lancaster.

❑ *From the station use the steps down to the by-pass, and take the minor road under the railway line. Passing Swaw Beck Farm it rises to a junction. Take the narrower branch left, and in 100 yards keep left up a rough walled lane.* At once look back to enjoy the start of near-permanent views back over the Ribble to Settle's limestone hills, backed by Rye Loaf Hill and the long line of Fountains Fell. *The lane runs into a field.* From the gate look back to find Penyghent entering the scene above the scar of Giggleswick Quarry, while further left, Ingleborough's classic outline appears in splendid isolation. Also prominent is the copper dome of the chapel at Giggleswick School.

Cross to the far corner with a line of telegraph poles, to find a corner-stile leading to a gateway onto reedy Cocket Lane. Turn up it, encountering the dampest part of the walk as it accommodates a small stream. A good prospect of Rome Crag is seen to the right. *Emerging into a broadening, rough pasture at the end, rise by the left-hand wall to a brow.* With stony ground extending west from the Rome Crag group, here is the first forward prospect, with colourful open country promising much.

As the wall turns away, Cocket Moss appears below. The view now features our goal, though this first sighting of Whelp Stone Crag's flat top suggests it's a heck of a way! **Bear left above the moss and drop to a gate, from where a solid track bridges the mire to a stony brow behind. A thin trod, initially marshy, continues away, fading but pointing the way to a long, straight wall.** Over to the right are the distinctive Birchshow Rocks. **Arriving exactly at a stile, go through and down the field, negotiating a fence before locating a two-slab footbridge over a tinkling stream. From a stile behind, rise up the field to a similar stile 30 yards to the right of a gate to join a narrow lane.**

Map labels:
GIGGLESWICK
station
railway
Birchshow Rocks
Rome Crag
Sandford
Giggleswick Common
Cocket Moss
① ⑨ Littlebank
⑩
② ⑧ Swainstead
③
Rathmell Common
Gisburn Forest
Scoutber Crag
④
Rathmell Beck
⑦
Whelpstone Lodge
⑥
Hesley Hall
⑤ Whelp Stone Crag 1217
N

Turn right, enjoying an uncluttered prospect of Penyghent, but with nearby Birchshow Rocks providing the best feature. **Passing a couple of farm drives, the road emerges onto the open common. From a brow the road drops again to become enclosed at Sandford Farm. The footpath enters the yard, along the front of the house, and from a gate on the left slants across the field to a stile back onto the common.** With less disturbance, one might simply turn directly onto the common to follow the wall the few yards up to the stile.

A better track climbs a few yards out from the reedy wall-side. At the next wall-junction above, it bears away from the wall across the common, levelling out beneath a bracken bank. Ahead is the forest edge, and the crest of Whelp Stone Crag re-appears. **Much nearer are ruins of a shooting lodge, to which a thin green path breaks off.**

The main way runs on a little further but fades quickly. Either keep on to an old shooting butt, then turn sharply left down to a fellow one by Dubs Beck; a little earlier, a clear sunken way rakes down to this same point. Cross the beck's reedy environs and head away, a trod working a way past a line of old butts, aiming for the skyline trees. Over to the right is the prominent knoll of Foxholes Crag.

Winter on
Whelp Stone
Crag,
looking to
Ingleborough

Bearing gently right, a parallel line of butts lead up a dry and clearer way to pronounced sunken ways on the near brow. Here the mass of Gisburn Forest appears, giving a first real sense of its scale. Up to the left the long top of Whelp Stone Crag makes its presence known. **Our path winds pleasurably on towards the trees, fading before them** somewhere on the unmarked county boundary. **Without reaching the trees turn sharply for the near forest corner up to the left. A faint green track forms to run towards it, becoming a well-made way to rise, ultimately sunken, to the forest corner.** Turn to savour this grand location, ensconced in rich upland colour.

Through the gateway, step over the fence on the left and head up the forest edge. In time we are ushered outside the old wall, and over a brow. The crag increases in dominance, while unplanted forest reveals the Bowland fells over to the right. **Underneath the nearest craggy bluff the way swings towards the forest, entering it, briefly, at a corner. A gap in the wall and a fence-stile see us on a level course. At the end turn left with the wall - still inside these rogue upper plantings - to gain the western rim of the crag.**

Though Whelp Stone's crest is just above, the right of way remains outside the fence. Turn down to the right with it through a tangle of rocks and trees, a discarded millstone reposes at the base of the rocks. *Still inside the forest edge, fence and old wall head away from the crag to a gate out of the forest onto unkempt Holden Moor. Double back across the pathless moor to the base of the crag. The right of way continues along the base to a gateway at the far end. Those detouring to the crest - as many do - should bear in mind they are venturing onto private land, and act with due responsibility.*

The summit of Whelp Stone Crag is a most extensive viewpoint. Its OS column (S5620) is insignificant, however, as one is drawn to the craggy northern rim. The panorama boasts: to the west, Bowland's steep slopes and rounded tops beyond Stocks Reservoir; Pendle Hill to the south-east with a battery of South Pennine heights beyond, and a fine array of Dales mountains nearer to hand. Seldom known by name, Whelp Stone Crag is a prominent landmark from the A65. Heading north from Long Preston, its long, flat-topped outline sits distinctly on the skyline across the Ribble.

A thin path runs east along this well-defined edge, and as a crumbling wall comes up, a gateway appears ahead in a solid wall. Dropping down either side of this returns to the right of way, which runs through a gateway at the foot of the slope. From the gateway a track runs above the wall-side to a gate by a small fold beneath the last knoll. From it aim for an obvious gateway, but then bear left with the wall. From its corner turn down the pasture to a similar corner below. Pass through the gate to descend a track to Whelpstone Lodge. Turn down its yard and out along the access track, which quickly becomes surfaced. Here, high profile Scoutber Crag over-rides the more distant Dales interest.

Since leaving the forest behind on our invisible path across Holden Moor, we have traced an ancient way from Bailey Lane, above Tosside, to Rathmell: from here-on surfaced and known as Old Oliver Lane, *the road is followed for a further mile, traffic-free, downhill and with grand views. Passing two farms, a junction is reached. Go left, bound for Rathmell.* Opposite the drive just ahead, a milestone at the base of the wall bears a well weathered inscription, possibly referring to the three miles to Tosside.

Millstone, Whelp Stone Crag

Continue a little further, and immediately before Hesley Hall, the next farm, take a walled way on the left. This runs on as a fine promenade overlooking lower country to the Dales hills. On the brow take a stile on the right, and slant left to locate a well-hidden stile in the descending wall. Slant down the bouldery pasture to the rear of a barn, take the left-hand gate to descend a large pasture to the foot of the wall on the left. Here a little bridge crosses Rathmell Beck in a lovely setting. Rise directly away up the bank to another stile at the far corner. On through an oval enclosure, bear right and up by wall and fence-side to a gate onto a lane.

Go left 200 yards then right along a superb green way between walls, Swainstead Raike. On the brow Settle returns to the scene beneath its hills. At the end the track bears right, down to a no-mans-land. Don't rise to the farm, but go left to a gate across a tiny stream. A green rake bears right above the beck, then a pathless way runs atop the wooded bank. This big, stony pasture is Coney Garth. From a stile in the wall at the end, enter a pocket oakwood, bearing left out of it to contour on to a fence-stile. Keep straight on across the field to approach the impressive house of Littlebank.

Its drive is joined but not followed in, as a stile admits to its wooded outer garden. Descend along the foot to a kissing-gate in the far corner. Cross the big field well to the right of a barn, to a stile where wall and fence meet. Head away to the left-hand of two barns, and from a wall-stile continue with the left-hand wall to a gate and stile, then straight across to another stile. Advance over a low brow with the wall, taking a stile near the end to cross a field corner to the next. Cross to another into the last field with the station just ahead. A stile at the far corner leads to the road under the railway bridge to return to the station.

Looking north past Scoutber Crag to Ingleborough and its satellites, Simon Fell and Park Fell

104

(22)

THE SALTERS WAY

START Slaidburn   Grid ref. SD 713523

FINISH Hornby (or Wray)

DISTANCE 15 miles

ORDNANCE SURVEY MAPS
1:50,000
Landranger 97 - Kendal to Morecambe
          103 - Blackburn & Burnley
1:25,000
Outdoor Leisure 41 - Forest of Bowland & Ribblesdale

ACCESS Start from the war memorial in the village centre.
Slaidburn is served by bus from Clitheroe and occasionally
Settle. Hornby is served by Lancaster-Settle buses. If returning
by train, consider a finish in Wray, from where Wennington
station is easily reached. If transport can be left at each end,
then road walking can be severely pruned: surfaced roads
occupy the first 3 and the final 4 miles.

The road walking is, however, largely traffic-free, and only a
complete crossing captures the full spirit of the walk. Perhaps
the best way is to get a lift to Slaidburn, ideally from Settle or
Giggleswick stations, and then return by rail from Wennington.

*Described by various trampers throughout the century as one of the
finest moorland crossings in England, the Salters Way is an
essential inclusion, notwithstanding logistical problems. A light-
weight pair of boots is a real boon, as it includes a high proportion
of hard surface. Also, wait for a clear day - there might be a lot of
history to this walk, but there are also a lot of views!*

Linking the Lune and Hodder valleys, the Hornby Road - or Salters Way - has for centuries been a busy moorland highway. It is best known as a salters' packway from Morecambe Bay to the farms of the Ribble Valley: the name Salter Fell, further west, recalls those days. Happily its surface has remained untarmaced for many miles over the moors, leaving a classic walkers' way. For several miles it overlays a Roman road.

For some notes on Slaidburn, refer to WALK 1.

☐ **Leave by the road past the** Hark to Bounty **inn, a steep hill** which at the top affords excellent views of the fell country ahead. **The road undulates for another mile or so,** passing Ellerbeck Hall with its 1694 datestone. **A junction with Woodhouse Lane is reached:** note the old guidepost, inscribed Slaidburn, Hornby, and 1816. Both hall and guidepost are illustrated in WALK 2. **Turn right along here, now undulating again for a while.** At a bend at the drive to Mytton Farm Crafts, note the base of a wayside cross on the verge. Known as the Cross of Brown, it was one of a number that lined monastic routes.

A swing left precedes a steeper climb onto the fell. Just before the fell-gate, stop at the top of the belt of trees and look over the wall. A slender ditch rising through the field is the line of the Roman road from Ribchester to Over Burrow in the Lune Valley: we shall soon be joining it. **The tarmac ends at the gate, and a concrete surface takes over the running.**

R. Wenning
R. Hindburn
HORNBY
WRAY
Moor Lane
River Roeburn
Claughton Moor
Thornbush
Barkin Bridge
Lower Salter
Middle Salter
Higher Salter
Goodber Fell
River Roeburn
Mallowdale Pike △ 1420'
Salter Fell
Mallowdale Fell
'county gate'
White Hill 1785' △
Wolfhole △ Crag 1729'
Hard Hill Top
Whitendale River
Croasdale Fell
Baxton Fell 1538' △
Croasdale Brook
Dunsop Fell
Higher Wood House
R. Hodder
SLAIDBURN

N

The Cross of Brown

Striding out, enjoy views back over a wide landscape, including Stocks Reservoir and Pendle Hill. **Running on above Croasdale, the old road swings left to enter fell country proper.** Here the Roman road comes in, to be overlaid for three miles by our road. Together they are seen climbing past an old quarry high on Croasdale Fell.

A slight descent to New Bridge precedes a climb beneath the quarry. At the bend above, easier going becomes the order of the day, with the upper reaches of Croasdale outspread. Dark heather moors on our left contrast with grassier slopes across the brook. A shooting house is passed on the left, while across to the right the rockfields of Great and Little Bull Stones decorate the flank of White Hill. **The track gradually approaches the Croasdale-Whitendale watershed fence,** and the view opens to reveal the rocky crest of shapely Wolfhole Crag. At 1365ft the fence marks the summit of the road, despite the major watershed not yet being reached.

Level walking ensues as the surface softens, a short section being ruined by vehicular use. Along the head of Whitendale, its full length reveals a range of fells presided over by the dome of Totridge. Ahead, meanwhile, Mallowdale Fell, fronted by its Pike, stretches beyond Wolfhole Crag. By the time **the old county boundary fence is reached at 1345ft,** the Roman road has parted company by striking off to the north. All waters previously flowed south-east to the Hodder, but from here-on, by way of the Roeburn, they flow north-west to the Lune.

Whernside and Ingleborough from Alderstone Bank

107

A harder track returns, and the high level walk across Salter Fell runs for some time before gaining the crest of Alderstone Bank. Interest increases on arrival at the arrangement of scattered rocks. The first group of rocks offers the first chance of any shelter for several miles, but more importantly heralds the onset of views out to the north. Three Peaks country is awaited with baited breath, and once gained, will largely remain in our sights for the rest of the walk. A greater collection of rocks is reached at the end of the brow, and just beyond, a well-made shooters' track slants down to cross

WHERNSIDE   INGLEBOROUGH   PENYGHENT

The Three Peaks of Yorkshire from Middle Gate

the river. **Now begins a pronounced descent of Alderstone Bank,** paralleling the deep trough of the youthful Roeburn backed by the great wall of Mallowdale Fell: isolated Mallowdale Farm may be discerned on its lonely knoll. Far ahead are Morecambe Bay, and the Lakeland Fells beyond the Lune Valley.

High Salter Close is entered, and then left at Middle Gate (with a crumbling bield in evidence on the left), **and thence down to finally reach the outpost of High Salter Farm,** first habitation since Higher Wood House almost 9 miles back. Those with transport arranged may have finished, but Hornby is a further 4½ miles on country roads. An alternative finish in Wray can pick up WALK 17 from High Salter, for less road walking.

High Salter

The Hornby Road heads down past the farm and two further Salter hamlets to the lovely setting of Barkin Bridge, our only meeting with the Roeburn. Beyond, the road cruelly demands one further pull before a long, level stride. One of several farms passed is the Middle Wood Centre, an organic farm promoting environmentally aware land use and building design. It has a new study centre, and runs various courses. *The moor is left at a cattle-grid at Whit Moor Gate.* Just past it, note an indecipherable milestone set into the wall on the right. *The final leg is downhill into Hornby,* though a right branch offers a second chance to finish in Wray. A last pause is on offer on a seat adjacent to an old roadside cross. *A final descent to Butt Yeats precedes crossing the B6480 to enter Hornby.*

Hornby is a neat village, lots of attractive stone houses lining the main street, split by the wide Wenning rolling through for its final mile to the Lune. Resplendant from the bridge is Hornby Castle, which is not open to the public. The original castle dated from Norman times, and after a Royalist defence during the Civil War, Cromwell had it dismantled. It was rebuilt in the mid-19th century, though apparently parts of a 13th century tower remain. St. Margarets church also has an intriguing tower, an octagonal one dating from 1514. In the porch are fragments of Anglo-saxon crosses, including the famous 'loaves and fishes cross'.

Barkin Bridge,
Roeburndale

SOME USEFUL ADDRESSES

Ramblers' Association 1/5 Wandsworth Road, London SW8 2XX
Tel. 0171-582 6878

Lancashire Countryside Service (Bowland AONB)
PO Box 160, East Cliff County. Offices, Preston PR1 3EX
Tel. 01772-264709

North West Water (Recreation & Conservation Officer)
Pennine House, Stanley Street, Preston PR1 4EA
Tel. 01772-822200

Tourist Information
12-14 Market Place **Clitheroe** BB7 2DA
Tel. 01200-25566

Discovery Centre, Council Offices, High Street **Garstang** PR3 1FU
Tel. 01995-602125

The Guildhall, Lancaster Road **Preston** PR1 1HT
Tel. 01772-253731

Town Hall, Cheapside **Settle**, North Yorkshire BD24 9EJ
Tel. 01729-825192

29 Castle Hill, **Lancaster** Lancashire LA1 1YN
Tel. 01524-32878

8 Station Road, **Bentham** North Yorkshire LA2 8JD
Tel. 015242-62549   (seasonal)

Yorkshire Dales National Park Centre Clapham
Tel. 015242-51419

Bowland Camping Barns YHA, 16 Shawbridge Street, Clitheroe,
BB7 1LY Tel. 01200-28366

Lancashire County Transport Information
County Surveyors Dept, PO Box 9, Winckley House, Cross Street,
Preston PR1 8RD   Tel. 01772-254868

British Rail, Skipton-Lancaster line Tel. 0113-244 8133

LOG OF THE WALKS

WALK	DATE	NOTES
1		
2		
3		
4		
5		
6		
7		
8		
9		
10		
11		
12		
13		
14		
15		
16		
17		
18		
19		
20		
21		
22		

INDEX

Principal features: walk number refers